OUR SELVES

100 MICRO MEMOIRS

EDITED BY LAURA KEENAN
AND CASEY MULDER

First published in 2024 by
NIGHT PARROT PRESS
Perth 6000
Western Australia
www.nightparrotpress.com

Copyright text © individual authors, 2024
The moral rights of the creators have been asserted.

This book is copyright. Apart from any fair dealing for the purpose of private study, research, criticism or review, as permitted under the Copyright Act, no part may be reproduced by any process without written permission. Enquiries should be made to the publisher.

Edited by Laura Keenan and Casey Mulder
Cover design by Mali Merttens
Typeset in Adobe Garamond by Lasertype
Printed by Advance Press, on recycled stock

A catalogue record for this book is available from the National Library of Australia

ISBN: 9780648706366 (paperback)

Department of
Local Government, Sport and Cultural Industries

Publication of this title was assisted by the State Government through the Department of Local Government, Sport and Cultural Industries.

Night Parrot Press is an independent publisher of non-traditional works of fiction and non-fiction.

Night Parrot Press acknowledges the Wadjuk Noongar people as the spiritual and cultural custodians of Boorloo and the boodja on which we publish. We honour and respect First Nations stories and express our gratitude for this heritage of powerful storytelling.

Introduction

When we think of memoir, we often envision a hefty tome of ephemera: diary entries, letters, photos, a catalogue of a life along a timeline of chronological order. But what happens when we zero in on the moments just outside the frame in family slideshows or videos, or edited from the carefully selected histories we tell about ourselves? With this anthology, we weren't interested in traditional milestones or podium accomplishments, nor were we moved by tales with satisfying endings or punchlines. The micro memoirs in this collection instead focus on interactions, incidents, and observations seemingly insignificant but monumental in their pain, reflection and joy, sharing universal truths through a very personal lens.

Ourselves: 100 Micro Memoirs is the first anthology by Night Parrot Press that celebrates creative nonfiction. With this departure from our previous collections of flash fiction, we felt an even greater sense of responsibility to honour the authors who shared their true stories with us. Writing and publishing something personal requires a different kind of courage than writing fiction. Launching into waters of real life, for fiction writers especially, can feel like sailing without a life jacket. Memoir is raw and messy and chaotic, reflecting our real lives.

Introduction

Like its literary cousins flash and microfiction, micro memoir requires writers to choose words carefully when constructing their story. The writers in this anthology had a limit of 750 words, which is a bit cruel when trying to distil a life. But micro memoir doesn't aim to condense an entire life. Its focus is much smaller—a moment or incident or conversation—which grows in significance when projected on a larger scale. For those of us old enough to remember slide shows, the excitement of seeing holiday memories or family gatherings on a big screen was magical. Each memory, framed on a miniature slide, waited its turn in the mechanical circle, clicking ever closer to the light source until its five or ten seconds of fame. Usually, a parent or teacher arranged the order and held the remote, controlling our experience of these memories. With micro memoir, writers hold the remote and project the memory, letting a moment linger far longer on the page.

This collection contains voices that hold us in awe. Each story is unique, but there are beautiful threads of shared experience that resonate across cultures and generations. From grief and loss to love and heartbreak, to school and childhood moments that have shaped us; from siblings and family we have known or never known. There are stories of place—home, the sea, nature, as well as locations we have travelled to. There are animals who have brought comfort or inspired imagination, and objects that physically represent specific occasions or people. There

Introduction

are also stories of our bodies and how they hold markers of our identities—physical and emotional—over time.

Making a book is like organising a family gathering, except everyone wants to be there. We thank the 100 writers who have trusted us with their stories—we admire each one of you and are thrilled that your story gets its glory on the page. We also thank the Western Australian funding body, Department of Local Government, Sport and Culture, for providing the grant to publish this anthology. Keith Feltham deserves a sainthood (granted in a lifetime supply of sour snakes) for his unmatched typesetting skills and patience. Mali Merttens has created the cover of our dreams, magically combining our wild ideas into a nostalgic yet modern work of art. Linda Martin, although not an editor on this project, has provided her wisdom and invaluable support, keeping us on track and performing tasks when she really should have been concentrating on her PhD—we love you, Linda! Thanks to our proofreader Sally Martin, for her impeccable eyes. And lastly, we would also like to thank our Night Parrot Board who provided sound guidance as we navigated the production of this collection, our fourth anthology and sixth book to date. We look forward to continuing to push boundaries with genre and form, connecting with new audiences and providing exciting platforms for emerging and established writers.

Laura Keenan and Casey Mulder, editors

Contents

Introduction — v

Contents — ix

AVRIL MULLIGAN
Big Place — 1

SCOTT-PATRICK MITCHELL
School Spirit — 3

KATHERINE ALLUM
Animals of the Mojave Desert — 7

CINDY SOLONEC
Boarding — 12

ISABELLE BIONDI SAVILLE
Tanked — 16

NICKI BLAKE
The Day Elvis Died — 18

BELINDA ROWE
Our Strong Young Hearts — 20

REBECCA M. NEWMAN
Sixteen — 23

JUDI LANE
Beginnings — 25

Contents

ALISON DAVIS
Bullets and Bracelets — 27

TEENA RAFFA-MULLIGAN
To Tell the Truth — 29

W. J. ARTHUR
Hidden in Plain Sound — 33

TRACY PEACOCK
The Empty Chair — 36

DAVID ALLAN-PETALE
Parma's Life of Minor Crimes — 38

SABRINA DUDGEON-SWIFT
Blak No Sugar — 41

SHARRON HOUGH
Hey Little Hen — 43

MELINDA TOGNINI
Tree House — 45

MELANIE HO
The Train to Heidelberg — 48

JESSE GALEA
Late to the Party — 51

ALEXANDER THORPE
A Non-exhaustive Review of Things that Have Been Yelled at Me from the Window of a Holden Commodore — 55

CAROL MILLS
The Camp Follower — 57

Contents

JESSICA BOWKER
In Absentia — 60

CARMEN COSGROVE
All Women — 63

ROCHELLE PICKLES
The Great Storm — 65

SALLY THOMAS
Ourselves, a Muted Frequency — 68

ANNIE HORNER
That Coat — 71

BARRY DIVOLA
Free of the Earth — 73

ZOE DELEUIL
The Nit Note — 77

TESS ALLEN
Racing Heart — 81

SARAH MOREDOUNDT
Jasmine and Nostalgia — 84

TIFFANY HASTIE
Sighted Swallow Swarm — 86

AKSEL DADSWELL
Where Does All that Sorrow Go? — 89

ROS THOMAS
A Man in a Van — 92

ANGEL HAYWARD
Stuck — 96

Contents

EM READMAN
Viewfinder — 97

CORAL MONTERO LOPEZ
Escapisms — 100

ELLIE COTTRELL
My Sister, the Mythical Creature — 103

AMBER MOFFAT
Pain(t) — 106

WILL YEOMAN
Holy Family — 109

SHARRON BOOTH
Share House Story — 111

ANGE YANG
Half-baked History — 115

RACHELLE ERZAY
A Limestone Cottage, with a Skylight to the Stars — 119

DANIELLE BERRYMAN
Wouldn't You Rather Be in the Kitchen? — 121

GREIG JOHNSTON
London Brawling — 124

GILLIAN O'SHAUGHNESSY
A Medley of Love Songs — 128

BRODI SNOOK
Forever Eleven — 131

Contents

PIA RUSSO
Are Three Underpants Enough? — 134

MABEL GIBSON
The Day He Died — 135

LOUISE BURLINSON
Summer, 1981 — 136

YING XIONG (DAVID) GOH
The Unfortunate Die Twice — 138

LAUREN MCLENNAN
My Letterbox — 141

KYEESHA BONNEY
139 Yale Rd — 143

PHILIPPA FREEGARD
The Window — 144

ALICE MACRI
Austerity — 147

ANDREW TETLAW
Sunday Gherkins — 150

SHANNON BRIE
The Last Pieces — 151

ANA LYNCH
Notes of J.C.L. — 155

SETH MALACARI
The Water Cycle — 157

CAROLINE HAYWARD
Where It Began — 161

Contents

SHIRLEY MARR
The Prosperous Red Phoenix Restaurant   164

GRACE JUNIPER GOODWIN
Dust and Ashes   167

KAYLEE MCINTYRE
Frenchman Bay My Father,
Frenchman Bay My Mother   170

RACHEL MCELENEY
Summer Days   174

MELANIE HOBBS
Saaptiya?   175

MARTIN LINDSAY
Hunger Games   177

ASHA BURNETT
Beach Body   180

SEAN MURPHY
The Gym Horse   182

SUSAN MIDALIA
Grounds for Dismissal   186

JAY CHESTERS
Hutt Lagoon, Pink Lake   188

ALISON MIDDLETON
The Bluest Skies   189

K. T. DOWNS
Bees   191

Contents

MIRIAM FISHER
They Watch — 194

DONNA MAZZA
I Woke Before Dawn Thinking of Wagin — 197

ELLEN O'BRIEN
Exhalation — 201

CHRISSIE HORLEY
Shattered Expectations — 203

RASHIDA MURPHY
Transgression — 204

ALASTAIR MCLEAN
Brushstrokes in the Shape of Us — 207

MARK KEENAN
Advantage Receiver — 208

EMILY TSOKOS PURTILL
On the Other Side Is Antarctica — 211

LESLEY MCKAY
Sisters — 214

RICHARD ROSSITER
The Back Lane — 217

SHANNON FARRELLY
Don't Oversell It — 221

ALYSSA SHAPLAND
A Long-standing Love Affair with Kisschasy — 225

JOSEPHINE TAYLOR
Upsy Down Town — 228

Contents

SALLY MURPHY
Mistaken Identity — 231

LAURA MOTHERWAY
Women in Waiting — 234

CAITLIN PRINCE
Canon — 237

JUDD EXLEY
The Second Frog — 240

ANA BRAWLS
The Timekeeper — 242

CLAIRE STEWART
The Beginning of the End — 245

SERGE TOUSSAINT
My First Apple, 1954 — 248

GUY SALVIDGE
Helicopter Parents — 251

ROSEMARY SAYER
The Mustard Pot — 254

JOEL HUEY
Waterfall — 256

THERESA WILKS
Horse — 259

EMILY RAINSFORD
Collaboration with Light — 261

MARIA PAPAS
The Man on the Driveway — 264

Contents

ASHA RAJAN
Learning to Swim   268

VIKI CRAMER
The Shells   272

CAROLINE JUNIPER
Open Studio   275

Editors   277

Contributors   279

Big Place

Avril Mulligan

At the bottom of the hill waits the bay. It's a small bay, deep, and the sand holds the tiniest, most perfect shells. I've spent many hours, on other days, combing the sand for them with my fingers; lining them up in order of colour and size, taking them home in small jars. Once, when my stepson was small, he sifted the sand with me, winter sun on our backs. He waits now with the rest of them at the bottom of the steep curving path.

The peppermint trees that line the path are old and craggy. Their bark is rough but their leaves are elegantly long and slender. The path is dusty dirt and I am wearing impractical shoes. We thought about wearing hiking boots; we laughed about that. But here we are, in the end, with our smart shoes in the dust.

Under the big sky, I take your hand. This is exactly where we have chosen to be. Amongst the sounds and the smells and the inconvenient wind; amongst the small tribe of our people. When we round the bend and see them waiting, nestled below the big rocks of the bay, I cry. This is a big place. Our small moment is playing out within it.

Avril Mulligan

We take our position under the makeshift huppah, at the edge of the noisy waves, at the edge of this land that we belong to. The rings that we will place on each other's finger are in my sister's hand. We are not young, and this is not our first time.

High up on the cliffs above the bay, someone takes our photo, and later we see the picture of ourselves—tiny specks spread across the white sand of the rocky bay.

School Spirit

Scott-Patrick Mitchell

Eight is such a brilliant age, full of reckless certainty. For me, this bravado manifested at the Summer Swimming Carnival. Actually, it surfaced a fortnight prior, at sign-ups.

'Freestyle relay anyone?' Mr Taylor asked the restless, smelly PE class.

Freestyle: my mind raced. Free. Style. Any style in the world. Any! The glorious swooping of a butterfly. The laidback log with waterwheel-armed grace of backstroke. The frog-like ribbit-swim of breaststroke. Or—and here my brain waterfalled into a torrent of possibilities—I could come up with an extraordinarily efficient and totally new swimming style, the likes of which the world had never seen. And would most likely gasp at, feel faint, and lay down after witnessing.

That, or I could do the style I had been practicing in the pool at home.

I put my hand up, too eager for my own good.

'Mitchell?' Mr Taylor's bushy eyebrows arched over his square-framed glasses. 'Are you sure?'

I nodded.

'It's ok, Mr Taylor, he's from Watson and they never win,' someone called out and everyone laughed.

It's true: my house never won. Anything. Ever. Maybe the maths contests. But for sports, we always came last. Always. It was our honour. Our prestige. Had been a fact for so long I believe the school invented the maths contests just so Watson could win something.

But this year was going to be different. I was single-handedly going to lead Watson to victory with my glorious 'free style' swim. I would become a legend. The glory of the school. I'd be in the papers, on TV. Heck, The Queen herself would want to meet me, such was my bravado.

I realised I was in trouble when the Freestyle Relay started and the more athletic boys from the other houses began that horribly graceful arm-swooping, head-turning swim. *Oh*, I thought, *THAT's what freestyle is*. I loathed freestyle. Hated it with all my being. Who could possibly be coordinated enough to execute that without a lung full of chlorine. Not me.

'Ummm, Mr Taylor,' I called, dressed only in the sad blue swimming togs that were the colour of Watson. 'I don't think I can do this.'

'Nonsense, Mitchell. Just do your best.'

I was the last relay swimmer. I watched as every other boy executed the freestyle flawlessly. Well, every other boy except all three of my Watson housemates, who spluttered and flailed and lagged. By the time the final

School Spirit

relay swimmer had reached me, all the other houses had already finished.

I dove in. Emerged, head above the water, determined to swim like an Olympian doing ... the doggy style.

The entire swimming carnival fell deathly silent as I splashed and garbled my length of the pool, paddling like a drowned puppy. Mr Taylor's jaw dropped. The skeletal and sombre headmaster shook his head. And I paddled. Like Lassie. Like Toto. Like Rin Tin Tin.

From the sidelines of the pool, a black shape came bounding up. A scribble of black curled fur. Scruffy, our school dog. He ran up to the water's edge, looked me in the eye as I struggled to keep my head above water, and he let out a long howl in solidarity. And then he barked, loudly. And kept barking, following me as I swam. And as Scruffy barked, the crowd began chanting my name. And as the dog yapped, and the crowd chanted, my fellow housemates began whooping and clapping. Amid a cacophony of noise, I reached the other end, lunged out of the pool and bowed furiously for the crowd.

Everyone stood, laughing, cheering, clapping. Scruffy circled me, sat down, and then howled again. I hugged him and he licked my face.

After the spectacle, Mr Taylor pulled me aside, red-faced and eyebrows furrowed.

'Never *ever* embarrass the school like that again, Mitchell!'

My eight-year-old chest puffed out. I looked him dead in the eye, and said, 'Well, maybe next time you should specify that freestyle doesn't mean we are free to choose any style we want.'

Before Mr Taylor could say a word, our gaunt, bald-headed headmaster strode over. He shook my hand.

'Well done, young man,' he said, peering down. 'While I can't exactly agree with your antics today, you've certainly shown exemplary school spirit.'

When they called my name later that day for the School Spirit Prize, Scruffy came up with me to claim my trophy.

Animals of the Mojave Desert

Katherine Allum

Desert Iguana
Dipsosaurus dorsalis

The first time I met Daniel, he put a lizard into my hands.
 A desert iguana, he clarified.
 The iguana's sharp eyes peered at me. I felt the flicker of its heartbeat against my thumb.

Gila Monster
Heloderma suspectum

My family had moved into the rental down the street, and Angela became my new bestie. Past experience with big brothers taught me they were moody and disinterested. Not Daniel.
 No visit was complete without a Steve Irwin-esque animal presentation. I was a captive audience—the Nevada desert was a foreign, prickly landscape, after living in the Pacific Northwest among pines and soft cushions of moss.
 Here there be monsters.

California King Snake
Lampropeltis getula californiae

He asked if I'd like to hold a snake and, without waiting, offloaded it—pristine white and black stripes—into my hands.

Just don't squeeze him.

Daniel held up his hand, showing a recent bloody wound on the pad of his palm.

Pale Kangaroo Mouse
Microdipodops pallidus

Once, he gave Angela and me a ride to get lunch. I lingered in the car and haltingly asked him to Reverse, our high school's Sadie Hawkins Dance.

Daniel smiled at me, gently. He was going with someone else, but he said thanks for asking.

Mortified, I tried to delete this memory.

Gambel's Quail
Callipepla gambelii

Daniel stood in the living room holding a plump quail. Its topknot, an inky apostrophe, wavered as it looked around.

Animals of the Mojave Desert

He'd hit it with the quad when riding in the desert—fortunately, it was only stunned. He kept it overnight and was off to reunite it with its family.

You can touch him, he said. The topknot goes *boing*.

With my index finger, I lightly stroked the quail's head. The topknot did indeed boing.

Mojave Rattlesnake
Crotalus scutulatus

Someday, girls stop playing with dolls and orchestrating iguana weddings. Families leave rental houses and move into their real houses. Besties go to high school, where they have different classes and activities.

Then I heard Daniel had cancer. The bad kind.

What do you do when you're sixteen, and the first boy you asked to a dance gets that sick?

Western Banded Gecko
Coleonyx variegatus

A few years before, it was Independence Day and our neighbour Tony had a stash of fireworks from the Indian Reservation.

At dusk, the oppressive heat of the day lingered. Kids ran on the street with sparklers. Daniel showed up and we sat on the tailgate of his truck, waiting for Tony to light 'em up.

I remember my father charging toward us, his bald head emerging from the dark.

Hey Brother Allum! Daniel waved.

Later, my dad told my mom he was about to let loose on the creep with the pick-up, but then realised it was Daniel.

Moapa Dace
Moapa coriacea

We sat side-by-side on a pool lounge while people shouted Marco and Polo. He was thin but his hair was growing back.

Hey Katie. He grinned his blue-sky smile. My cancer's gone.

Did I remember when I asked him to Reverse? He'd wanted to go with me, but he'd already been asked. Plus, I wasn't sixteen—a Mormon rule. But we would've had a great time, huh?

Greater Roadrunner
Geococcyx californianus

That was the last time I saw him—the cancer came back.

Animals of the Mojave Desert

I was sick with recurring strep and couldn't visit him in hospital. Did I send a card? I feel like I did. I should've done more. Bought a hazmat suit.

I should have been there for Angela.

Red-Tailed Hawk
Buteo jamaicensis

At his funeral, people stood in the doorway and sat on the floor.

Home is an hour outside of Las Vegas—you round the corner on the highway and the Valley expands in front of you.

Think of the shy wildlife.

The tiny hearts fluttering in the sand.

Boarding

Cindy Solonec

It was a hot afternoon in the isolated Kimberley town of Derby. The three women sat in front of a full-length mirror braiding their hair, smearing red lipstick, and daubing way too much perfume while sharing ideas and gossip. With a bed pushed against the flywire window, its shutters wide open to lure the occasional breeze, my cousin and I masked our giggles while pretending to nap. Later in life, I realised that it would have been better, had the Spanish invaded our country. At least everyone would have had a siesta. Not just us littlies.

'She can go to school. She's already seven. You must talk to the nuns,' Aggie counselled Mum with Phyllis nodding in agreement.

Auspicious words that drifted into our ears. Kerry, six weeks older than me, was already at school and I wanted to be there too.

'That new aeroplane. It went straight up in the air like this,' Phyllis angled her arm at the ceiling. 'Like a rocket.'

Aggie and Mum chuckled at their friend's exaggeration. They too, had witnessed the spectacle. It was 1960 and a Fokker F27 Friendship, a turboprop airline that would take Kimberley kids south to boarding

Boarding

schools, had recently been added to a fleet of Douglas DC-3s that serviced the West Australian run. Locals had gathered at the airport to bask in the glory of seeing the plane for the very first time.

My dad, a remarkably hardworking Spaniard, was out bush developing his sheep station. The year before, my parents had sent my older sister to boarding school 2,000 km south to Geraldton. Running a pastoral property didn't leave them time to homeschool us kids.

Mum heeded Aggie's words and by October I had joined my older brother at the Catholic hostel in Derby. Crammed in the manager's small, pale yellow windowless van with a dozen other kids, it was standing room only for the short journey to school. All I could see were shorts and skirts from which protruded scrawny black legs. When my brother became seriously ill with an undiagnosed ailment before the end of the year, our parents removed us. I'd hardly even started school.

He was whisked off to Geraldton in February 1961 and I boarded with Aggie. However, by the second term I found myself on the DC-3 with my siblings. A cool breeze greeted us as we stepped from the plane. I shivered and moved closer to my sister. We went straight to collect my uniforms from downtown. Standing in the main street, I stared at the huge two-story buildings across the road that seemed to engulf us. My little head turned every which way.

'Jacinta, do you want an ice-cream wedge?' My sister's gentle voice broke my gawking.

A thick slice of strawberry ice-cream wedged between two wafers looked delicious. But I was not well. Sure, I suffered from car sickness and Mum always carried Dexal, an anti-vomiting powder mixed with water, to settle me on long journeys. But now, I had no relief.

That first year was a dramatic departure from my early childhood trajectory—evident in my school reports. I failed everything. By the second year, I had improved considerably. Aboriginal English and Kriol were treated like any foreign language that needed to be stamped out, so I was taught the Art of Speech. I hated it. My parents placed unconditional trust in the nuns' decisions, and I spent more time in their care than that of my parents. For nine scholastic years, I was away at boarding school.

Kimberley kids didn't go home for short breaks. It was too far. So, I went to Mid West boarders' homes. I missed Easters on the station, where I'd see the sun dance across the sky and spawn pulsating tinges of colour through thin clouds. My parents promised it was a sure sign that Jesus had arisen. I might even glimpse Him being escorted by angels if I got up early enough. But I never did. Half believing them, I was content to suck on hard, icing-glazed Easter eggs.

Between station life and an all-girls boarding school constrained by dormitory living, the college fence and homesickness, I wondered whether my parents had been overprotective during my formative years. I lacked social skills. When my boarding years came to an end in 1969, I had mercifully overcome motion sickness and enjoyed

Boarding

air travel. Relief at last. Within four years and into the future, I confidently wandered abroad, discovering places far beyond my childhood.

Tanked

Isabelle Biondi Saville

It's something to do with her lungs. All I know is that she doesn't like hugs, or rather hugs squeeze all the air out of her body and make her feel like she's drowning. This is a feeling I understand, as I watch her slowly die. That's a secret we're keeping from each other, though. She pretends she's feeling a bit better than yesterday and I pretend to believe her.

She tells me that the oxygen makes her feel like she's carrying a scuba tank around with her. I have never seen my nonna at the beach, though I imagine her between the waves, weightless brown curls stretching across the Indian Ocean as she floats on her back.

I ask her if she's ever been? She tells me that she liked seeing the beaches on Rotto, but that she doesn't know how to swim. It's easy, I tell her. You just kind of move your arms like a windmill and kick. She laughs. When you're feeling a bit better, I say, I'll take you to the beach. She smiles. But I can tell by the way she squeezes my hand that we both know one day soon I'll walk in to find she's gone. Gone-gone, not just bed-empty-gone, though I'd rather that.

Tanked

I'd rather the nurses call and tell us that they've lost her. Literally, not figuratively. I'd rather turn on the TV to find the news reporting that a wild Italian woman broke out of hospital to brave the early morning swell at Mullaloo, oxygen tank abandoned in the dunes. I'd rather watch her stretching her arms like a windmill, hands slicing through the crisp, blue water as she turns her head to breathe.

The Day Elvis Died

Nicki Blake

At breakfast, the restaurant is quieter than usual. Some people are openly weeping over their coffee and pastries. Among the clinking of cutlery on china and muttered conversation, one word is noticeable in its repetition: Elvis.

The nice waiter, the one who speaks English, comes over to seat us at an available table. 'Elvis is dead,' he murmurs. Then, as if we are the family of the deceased, adds, 'Very sorry.'

He thinks we are American—most Romanians do. They talk about America a lot. The border guards demanded we give them 'American' blue jeans before they allowed us entry into the country. The local children stare when they see my brother and I drinking real Coca-Cola, which my father purchases with American dollars. The people I meet while accompanying my father on his business trip to Bucharest all talk about going to America one day.

I'm only six but I know it's hard for Romanians to leave their country, even though I don't really understand why so many of them want to. To me, it's a magical place of bitter chocolate ice-cream, grand buildings, and

The Day Elvis Died

a wide blue canal. I've never been to America, but I don't think it can be better than this.

Later that day, our car breaks down on a road which bisects a field of sunflowers. As my parents try to flag down passing cars, I look out at the vivid crop. The heavy blooms, wilting in the August sunshine, seem as downcast as the people at breakfast.

Eventually a car pulls up and the driver calls out in rapid Romanian. My father replies in loud, slow English.

The driver grins.

'American, yes?' Then his smile evaporates as he nods sympathetically and says, 'Elvis.'

Our Strong Young Hearts

Belinda Rowe

The school bus takes us out through the town centre, past the salt marshes to coastal country dotted with tall flax bushes and pohutukawa trees. The black sand glints in the morning sun and Jen and I chitchat about *Little House on the Prairie*. She asks me to do her hair in a French plait like mine, so I spend time brushing her long auburn hair until all the knots have gone. Mr Dickson tell us that on the excursion we'll be learning about supply chains—his words remind us of the daisy chains we make on the oval at lunch time.

The bus halts outside the white art deco facade of the freezing works, and we scramble behind Mr Dickson and his clipboard. In the front office we're greeted by a supervisor who seems like he'd rather be fishing. On the wall behind him is a 1975 Ford Fairlane Calendar—August's model is viper green with a black vinyl roof, the young woman posed on the bonnet wearing a short leather skirt, long white boots, and no top. She's staring straight at us.

Mr Dickson tells us it's killing season. The supervisor leads us through the clear plastic strip doors into the processing area where men in white overalls and black aprons scrape and cut with their sticking and skinning knives, flashing silver. We're struck by the cold, the drone of fans, men calling, and endless sheep carcasses without fleece, heads, or hooves, hanging like ghostly boxing bags from hooks. The smell of warm blood makes us gag. The man on our left has a wide smile and huge horsey teeth and is drawing out 85 feet of small intestine which he proffers to the class.

Mr Dickson clears his throat and begins with the first shipment of mutton and lamb in 1882 to London, then recounts the time of surplus when flocks were driven over cliffs into the sea, then his mouth moves breathlessly around the words supply and demand. Meanwhile, the small intestine lying on the bloodied concrete is stirring and slinking sideways to nuzzle against Jen's sandal and I feel her stiffen and smother a cry. I turn and whisper, *Mr Dickson's a real dick*. She grabs my hand and holds it tight and doesn't let go until we're outside.

We make our way to the back of the bus and slump onto the hard seat. I take out my sandwich and inspect it like I'm Jane Marple—luncheon sausage smeared with tomato sauce—and Jen inspects her sandwich and nods, her eyes downturned. I bundle them into the brown paper bag and drop it at my feet; it feels delicious to squash them real good. I nudge her with my elbow, and she wipes her eyes and smiles as I open the bus window, releasing our sandwiches into the southerly wind. They look like seabirds rising, their wings beating frantically against the gale, like our strong young hearts, and I put my arm around Jen and pull her close. She tells me her mum hasn't been home for sixty-three nights. She knows this because she's got the same Ford Fairlane Calendar at home and she keeps a record, crossing off the days, one after the other.

Sixteen

Rebecca M. Newman

The year I turned sixteen my bedroom was a chocolate box. The former owner of our new home had covered the house with offcuts, leftovers from her interior designer days. The floor of my room was carpeted with purple shag; the walls *and the ceiling* were resplendent in purple-blossomed wallpaper. I lay on my bed, the cloying wallpapered world closing in.

On weekdays I left the chocolate box to walk through a wetland to school, bag heavy on my shoulders. School was a rolling timetable, ever shifting, and twice a week: phys ed. Phys ed meant remembering an extra bag of clothes, relentless sun, fatigue. I had not yet been diagnosed with Hashimoto's. I just thought I was no good at sport.

I envied the kids who always had a note from home. The reasons varied—recovering from a migraine, stomach issues, plantar warts. It wasn't until years later I realised those kids wrote their own notes. Twice a week they got to sit together on the dead grass and watch the rest of us sweat.

The warm-up was always two laps of the oval—*Go!* A rule-follower, I never once cut the corners. I would trail the pack, legs cramping, and beat rhythms in my head to keep my body moving forward. Then, the division into teams. Two lean, confident kids selected for the day's captains took it in turns to build their teams from a motley crowd.

I sat and waited. I hated softball, soccer, hockey, the rule that the boys had to pass to two girls before trying for a goal. But I didn't want to be left till last—to be scrambling to stand with your team when they were already moving off.

I sat on scratchy grass under an oppressive sky and willed my name to be called.

Pick me.

Beginnings

Judi Lane

The pink and white striped dress is itchy. My bare, scabby knees stick out under the hem. Twitchy fingers worry a thread of a button. I need to go to the toilet so badly my stomach hurts and my head feels fuzzy. The shoes—black and shiny and new with silver buckles—are the most beautiful things I have ever seen. But they make me nervous. Knowing that I am the first one to wear them and keep them doesn't seem possible. Dragging my eyes away, I look up. My mouth goes dry. The people are still looking at me. I am five years old, and these are my new parents.

Fifty-nine years later, fragments of that day are viscerally clear, like watching a slide show: click the button and a scene appears—a raw moment bound in time, space and feeling. Click again, and the scene changes. In my mind's eye, I am still five, standing in the wardrobe room at the orphanage.

The room is functionally sparse. A single light bulb hangs from the ceiling, casting shadows on the faded green walls. Box shelving covers three walls. Each box holds a stack of sorted, neatly folded clothing, donated by a well-meaning community for the forgotten children of faceless, nameless women.

In the centre of the room is a tiered stand. Rows of scuffed shoes in varying sizes are slapped onto small feet here every morning. Today, the shoes are gone but the stand is not empty. It's groaning under the weight of a jumble of things.

Matron is talking to me. She is using her gentle but serious voice as she points to various objects. Somehow, all these treasures—the clothes, the books, the toys—belong to my brother and me. Until this point in time, I have owned nothing. The shoes worn on Monday are on someone else's feet on Tuesday. The only thing that has ever 'belonged' to me is my brother. The shoes drag my eyes down again. The fact that I now own them is almost too much for me to accept.

Finally, understanding sinks in. Today, we are leaving. Today, we get a family. Today, we get a real home.

I stare at the silver buckles as my feet take a shaky step forward.

Bullets and Bracelets

Alison Davis

My first love was the Bionic Man. But when Wonder Woman blazed across our screens, I was obsessed. She was everything I wanted to be. Fearless. Fair. Dressed in shiny lycra. I convinced my scrawny, ten-year-old self with chicken legs and a flat chest that I looked just like her. I imagined myself leaping into battle and flying my transparent plane. I was a mighty warrior and could deflect any danger with my magical wristbands. And then, like a snake slithering out from the shadows of the quadrangle, Kelly announced that she looked more like my idol.

It was game on. I rallied supporters, convincing students in our year to join my gang. She started recruiting followers throughout the school with the flair and confidence of a presidential candidate. When she broke her arm playing netball (well that's how I remember it, and I'm sticking to my story), I thought I'd won the lottery. Surely that would kick her out of the race. But still she persisted. Perhaps her accident even helped her campaign, attracting sympathy votes. We circled each other like wild cats. There was so much at stake, and neither one of us was willing to give up our superhero dream.

When I shoved her one day at school, she cried and said I'd hurt her injured arm. Questions were asked. Parents were called. There were stern discussions. In the interest of public safety, the school banned any further Wonder Woman warfare, and the gangs were disbanded. At once, I plummeted from gang leader and aspiring superhero to nerdy student.

I was disappointed, but in my heart I'd won. Her tears just proved she didn't have what it takes to save the world. And I knew what Wonder Woman would have said. *Make peace, not war.*

To Tell the Truth

Teena Raffa-Mulligan

'Mum can't lie.' It was one of my children's core beliefs about me throughout their growing years. I was compelled to tell the truth. Always. To do otherwise was unthinkable. Besides, I would give myself away. A flush of the cheek. A sliding glance. A nuance of tone or manner.

'Ask Mum,' they'd say. 'She always tells the truth.'

They didn't know about the little girl with the butterfly bow in short wispy hair who returned to class one day during her first year of school, breathless and happy after a lunch-break game of The Big Ship Sails Through the Alley-alley-oo with 'the big girls'. She was already a pleaser, a rule follower to the letter because that avoided trouble.

Once all the children were seated, the teacher stood in front of her desk and looked from one small face to the next, taking her time, letting every child know something serious was about to happen.

Her gaze settled on a little girl with bright eyes and an impish smile, and she beckoned with one finger. 'Come here, missy.'

The interrogation began. 'Did you go to the shop during lunch break?'

A nod.

'You know it is against the rules to leave the school grounds without permission.'

A small voice. 'Yes, miss.'

'You were seen. You weren't alone. There were two of you. Who came with you?'

Bright Eyes turned to point: 'She did.'

Butterfly Bow Girl jolted in her seat. It wasn't true. She'd spent the whole time in the lunch shed but the beckoning finger with the long scarlet nail couldn't be ignored.

Tummy churning, legs wobbly, she approached the desk.

The teacher stood over her. 'Did you go to the shop?'

Butterfly Bow Girl's tummy settled. There was nothing to worry about. All she had to do was tell the truth, like Mum said. She shook her head. 'No, miss. I ate my lunch and then I stayed in the shed and played with the big girls. I was with them. The whole time. Ask them. They'll tell you.'

The teacher's green eyes flashed. The coil of red hair on top of her head looked like a snake waiting to strike. 'Don't be impertinent. Go and stand in the corner until you're ready to tell the truth.'

'But I didn't—'

'Face the wall, please. We don't want to see little girls who tell lies.'

To Tell the Truth

Butterfly Bow Girl gulped back a sob. Tears pricked her eyes and slid down her cheeks. This wasn't fair. She hadn't lied.

Time seemed to crawl as she stood there. The lessons droned on. Eventually her tears stopped. She played with the folds of the pleated skirt her Italian grandmother had made her. The last time she'd worn it was the day everyone said the world would end. No one had said how or why that would happen, but she'd watched and waited in the schoolyard because it had felt like it might on such a day when the clouds were low and heavy and the sun didn't shine. The world hadn't ended then. She wished it would now. That would serve the teacher right for not believing the truth.

Butterfly Bow Girl chanced a glance at her, sitting at the desk marking papers. Would she make her stand here for the rest of the day? Long after the bell rang at home time and everyone else had gone?

'Miss—,' she said, her voice barely above a whisper.

The teacher looked up.

Butterfly Bow Girl took a breath and hoped God wasn't watching and listening the way Mum said He was when she told the lie: 'I did go to the shop at lunch time.'

So yes, despite what my children believe, I am capable of lying, especially when pushed into a corner. I would unhesitatingly lie to protect my loved ones. I also admit that I'm not always honest with myself.

I was telling the truth that day. I don't know why my classmate lied. To protect a friend? Get me in trouble?

Did she mistake me for someone else because we'd not long started school? And why did our teacher believe her and not me? She could easily have confirmed my story by speaking with the older girls I mentioned.

When I gave her the lie she wanted, she smiled triumphantly, convinced she'd taught me a lesson about honesty. What I learnt was that people don't always want to hear the truth.

Hidden in Plain Sound

W. J. Arthur

I have been walking a tightrope between two opposing worlds since I was six. I am adept at passing as one of the many, without people realising I belong to the few. They may have inklings, slyly suggested by my haughtiness. For the skilled observer, there is a fatal tell, the revealing detail under the poker face. Just watch, now, for the turning of the head.

Profound is a funny word.

Profound mysteries. Profound sadness. Profound knowledge. Profound deafness. Profound.

My right audiogram flatlines, skimming along the bottom like a stone.

Stone deaf. Deaf and dumb. Hearing impaired. Hard of hearing. Which epithet to choose?

I could be a foot away from the beautiful Rolls Royce engine of a 787 Dreamliner and I wouldn't hear a thing. Not one of the 140 decibels of roaring, straining engineering. A motorbike sits at around seventy, and a whisper slides in at a tiny thirty decibels.

My left ear is healthier, still a flicker of life, and it is in my left that I can hide, camouflaged, in the hearing world. When offered the choice of migrating into the hearing world for good, I took it.

For two months I cradled and nursed a secret close under my skull, hidden by twelve neat staples. The audiologists don't switch you on until you have healed. The ultimate in body modification, inching closer to a cyborg.

On the way home, after all of the smiles and thumbs up in the office, there were beeps and clicks and some tears. Nothing like the videos that loop on TikTok, where everyone is on an emotional high. It took a while for my sluggish brain to register that something was happening that hadn't been there before. No rejection of it, no tearing the thing off, no temper but little joy either. It was just a slow trickle of data. I walked, stiff necked like a turtle, swivelling my heavier head around without grace.

Then it came. God bless Harleys. On a perfect blue-sky day, with the window down, I was gifted a perspective by driving too slowly. A low rumbling, rising like a menacing crescendo. The crouching tiger donated an extra rev just at the right second. I could feel it too. Why hadn't I felt it before? Now the sound existed within me. The sound became mine. This was the signal my unworked nerves had been waiting for. The connection, the understanding, the desire to work. I was in harness and eager to pull the plough.

Hearing doesn't come for free. The sickly, atrophied nerves in my brain had to learn to work out, like a novice at the gym. Every day was leg day. I crawled through sounds. I now loved hard sounds. They were the easiest for me to pick up. P.I.C.K. U.P. Listen carefully. Decipher. A kettle of fish is not on the vocabulary list, but church is. The one word I heard clearly. Church. Church. Church. Was it a message?

Edging forward, I became a collector, obsessed with a library of sounds. Birds, drums, alarms all neatly catalogued and identified with the care of a scientist and the delight of an artist.

But jings, the hearing world is chaotic!

The Empty Chair

Tracy Peacock

It's been a couple of months since we last met. I set up our two folding chairs by the Canning River as usual, remembering our flowing conversations as we waited for the bottlenose dolphins to surface.

When we weren't searching for the playful pod, we'd watch for other wildlife. Sun-drenched cormorants amplifying their wings on a tree branch. Noisy seagulls sailing over the shimmering water. We'd fixate on our favourite pair of black swans plunging their endless necks into the water like head-standing yogis. I've read they have long and enduring relationships.

After a while, we'd settle back into our chairs and focus on our smooth flat whites. We'd sip. Laugh. Sip. Laugh some more. When the time was right, you'd take a breath and reveal the latest about the cancer.

Now, as I wait for my coffee to cool, I rummage through more memories shared across three decades of friendship. Becoming mothers. Birthday parties. Books. Watching tennis. Discussing Novak Djokovic. Christmas catch-ups. Cuddling puppies. Spaghetti marinara. Your recipe for lamb steaks with rosemary and sweet potato.

The Empty Chair

Today your chair remains empty as the waves mumble and I stare at the bloated blowfish belly-up on the shore. You'd warned me that we weren't going to share a future, talking rubbish and racing our walking frames. I should have believed you.

As I fold the chairs and prepare to go home, my bleary eyes scan our magical river one last time. If this was a fictional story, I know how we'd both like it to end. The dorsal fins would emerge, bodies shining like glazed ceramics, and we'd both go home happy. But that's not how true stories work.

Parma's Life of Minor Crimes

David Allan-Petale

We called my grandfather *Parma*, and I still refuse to believe he's dead. I prefer to anticipate that he'll knock on my door again soon and, eyes alight with mischief, ask if I want to come with him for a day where anything could happen.

He lived by three rules:
1. You can blag your way into anything
2. The very best is worth it
3. Judge an art gallery by what you'd steal.

Parma's mission in later life was to educate me and my sister 'before the Americans did'. He was a benevolent believer in the improving qualities of culture high and low. This fuelled an eternal search for the good stuff, whether inspecting newly harvested stone fruit at the Fremantle Markets, attending an opera in a box seat, or driving around in his sky-blue Mercedes to taste every pie in the annual top ten list.

While my school mates were busy at weekends, playing footy and watching cartoons, I had my own private Magwitch from *Great Expectations*, dressed head-to-toe in pressed khaki like his hero General McArthur,

Parma's Life of Minor Crimes

shirt pocket stuffed with cash for opening every door he could, by hook or by crook.

The routine was simple. He'd get up frightfully early on a Saturday morning and drive from his mid-century bungalow in Wembley Downs to my parents' brick-and-tile in Greenwood. There, he would knock at the door and my sister and I would answer, already dressed, ready to go.

'What are we doing today, Parma?' we'd ask.

'Pot luck,' he'd say, and off we'd go.

My favourite was watching the Whitbread Round the World Race yachts coming into Fremantle, and then going aboard to meet his friends who were crewing. Perhaps the funniest was a play where a scene of seduction was taking place on stage, and my sister asked, 'Parma, what's that man doing to the woman?'

'He's putting a spell on her,' was his quick answer, and a wisecrack behind said, 'Good save, Parma!'

One Saturday Parma arrived to speak with my parents, proposing to take me and my sister out of school for a six-week trip to Europe and the United States. He'd pay for everything bar our plane tickets, and all we had to bring was our bags and some 'iron rations'—muesli bars and snacks that we would resort to when funds grew tight.

London, Amsterdam, Munich and Berlin. A trip through the Alps, the canals of Venice and the ruins of Rome. We travelled across Europe in the same spirit as our Saturday trips, heading out each day to search down the very best things we could.

In Paris, right at the end of our Grand Tour, funds were tight. We'd eaten all the iron rations, and only had enough money to either visit the Louvre or go to Fauchon, arguably the greatest patisserie in the world.

We chose the pastries and ate them in sight of the Eiffel Tower—I still have the bag. But we'd miss seeing whether it was worth stealing the *Mona Lisa*, the *Venus de Milo*, *The Raft of the Medusa*, *Psyche Revived by Cupid's Kiss* …

'I know what to do,' Parma assured us, and we took the metro and emerged at the main entrance, where the queue was impossibly long. Parma kept walking, and we followed, knowing to trust his plans.

He led us all the way to the museum's gift shop where he cajoled a tired, frustrated guard to let him inside so that he could buy a book and left us outside to wait. After a few minutes, he came out again, looking distressed.

'I don't have my reading glasses with me,' he said to the guard. 'Would you allow my grandchildren in with me, so they can help?'

The guard threw up his hands, and in we went, playing along with Parma's elderly pantomime of browsing the art books. His senses sharpened when we reached the edge of the shop where a fence of stanchions divided commerce from art.

'Take your time,' Parma whispered, nodding to a gap, and beyond it the galleries, all ours to judge.

Blak No Sugar

Sabrina Dudgeon-Swift

I was the colour of a long, drawn-out cuppa tea with a splash of milk, but so was she.

Her backyard was small. Sweet citrus scents of the oranges and mandarins that lined the back fence glowed in the sunshine like baubles on a Christmas tree. She told us not to touch them and to stay outside. We played quietly—picking at the grass, trying to keep the grass stains off our new crisp dresses. Her round face and tight lips didn't move much as she chatted with Mum at the kitchen table.

I'm not sure how long we were there, but it was long enough to know we weren't welcome. Her stiff upper lip and beady eyes said it all. Did you know you can read a person by their eyes? She didn't have kind eyes. I never saw Great-Grandma Nell again.

Nell didn't approve of her granddaughter's life choices or the colour of her great-grandchildren. Even from a child's point of view it all seemed silly and without logic, as Nell's Indian mother had brown skin and her British father had white skin. My mother was white and my father was Aboriginal. As far as I could tell we were the same, the same cuppa tea except maybe hers didn't have sugar.

There was a man I remember too, with a little dog. He would visit our home from time to time, bring sweets and happily chat with Mum. He never stayed long. They were quick visits but I remember his kind eyes. Sidney was his name—my great-granddad who would visit us in secret.

Hey Little Hen

Sharron Hough

I wouldn't say I liked the sound of my own voice, but I did like to sing. In a household of judgemental siblings and no privacy however, my stage was limited.

At school I often wandered the perimeter of the playground singing made-up songs, careful not to look like I was talking to multiple personalities. It bought me a reprieve from being the target of brandy up on the asphalt or the taunts of being called a 'fat frog'—one of the more popular ice-creams at the time.

At home, the only place I could go to belt out a tune was the chook run. Yes, the chickens were a captive audience, but at least they flocked to my feet, seemingly mesmerised by my voice.

Their favourite show tune was 'Hey Little Hen' and though my stage smelt of chook manure, and flies volleyed themselves into my mouth whenever I opened it, I still managed to delight.

Peals of laughter from my siblings told me my stage had been discovered. I sent them running, chasing after them with my crazed groupies. I ushered my fans back from the gate and lured them with song like a terra-maid.

Quizzical faces watched intently as I bent forward, flies mobbing my eyes, when the mosh pit turned violent. I was struck by a beaked projectile. Perhaps not everyone thought it was a number one hit.

My eye streamed and feathers flew as I fled the crowd, locking the gate behind me. My other eye ran with tears in sympathy. Was it for my injury or was I hurt that my chickens had turned so judgemental?

I took the assault personally. It had been an eye opener, or closer—if you will—and it was a long time before I sang to any two-legged creatures again.

Life had flipped me the bird. It wouldn't be the last time.

Tree House

Melinda Tognini

The tuart tree squats on the grassy slope between our house and the chook shed, her strong arms outstretched. Her stocky physique makes it possible for ten-year-old me to climb up and into her branches. Our next-door neighbours have a prefabricated treehouse in their backyard; I improvise with the jarrah planks stacked against our asbestos fence, hoisting them up and wedging them in as best I can to form a rickety floor. The tuart's canopy suffices as a roof; walls seem an unnecessary complication. She becomes a refuge from the mean girls at school and the fight with my best friend during a sleepover, an escape from two younger brothers, a place to sulk after my parents have said no when I hoped they'd say yes.

Leaning back against her rough bark, weathered by many seasons before my arrival, I imagine the tops of her branches disappearing into the clouds like the magic faraway tree. Like the folk of the Enchanted Wood or Abigail slipping through time in Ruth Park's *Playing Beatie Bow*, books become my portals to other worlds and lives. Adventures in a smugglers' cove with the Famous Five. Seafaring in a pea-green boat with the Owl and the Pussycat. I experience grief alongside Wilbur and Charlotte, solve mysteries with Trixie Belden and Nancy Drew, undertake various implausible choose-your-own-adventures that inevitably result in my own demise.

And then the year I turn twelve, we embark on a family adventure of our own. We pack most of our belongings into boxes and stash them away in the garden shed. As we set off to criss-cross Australia, only the essentials make their way into our Landcruiser, which has been painted the colour of egg yolk.

'I'll be back,' I promise, wrapping my arms around the tuart's thick arms.

A false declaration.

We return only briefly the following Christmas before relocating to a remote mining town where my parents will teach maths and science. A year's absence stretches into five, ten, fifteen, twenty.

When I next walk through the side gate, it's to help my mother prepare the house for sale. The house is weary from years of renters, and the backyard is smaller than I remember, but it doesn't take me long to find my tuart or, at least, what remains of her.

After falling victim to termites, her heart hollowed out, tree-loppers have resorted to amputating her branches, leaving only a low stump. I bow my head in acknowledgement, as if pausing at an ancestor's grave.

In the shed, Mum and I sort through the boxes that remained behind when we moved. Sentimental mementoes to keep, household items for the op shop, the rest for the skip bin out the front.

The books of my childhood bear the scars of time. Those that aren't pockmarked by termites have been feasted on by silverfish or their pages curled with mildew. Most of them are destined for the skip. But I'm able to salvage a few: *The Folk of the Faraway Tree* and *The Enchanted Wood*, *Trixie Belden and the Mystery in Arizona*, *Choose Your Own Adventure: The Abominable Snowman*. As we disappear down the driveway one last time, I wrap my arms around these remnants and hug them to my chest.

The Train to Heidelberg

Melanie Ho

Before the train, a flight from Perth, an airport bus, a tram, the distraction of a profiterole tower. A slow Sunday gives way to Monday and now rush-hour commuters breeze past, eyes never leaving the station down the hill. They are not tempted by the stop-start of the trams, by the horns that express displeasure and impatience, by the halts and screeches tempered by an occasional good morning. But little legs that cannot keep up are accompanied by little eyes that wander, a little head that turns with every noise, with every voice.

He insists on holding his father's hand. The sidewalk cannot accommodate three across and so I hang back, a step behind, my own eyes trained on making sure his little hand does not slip from his father's grasp. He is in his good jeans and his good t-shirt, one that camouflages the protruding belly of low muscle tone. He walks steadily enough not to warrant a stranger's second glance; perhaps it is only a mother, a physiotherapist and a rheumatologist who notice the gait, who know there are black orthotics lining the insoles of his sneakers.

It is Melbourne in late September. 'Djilba,' he says, and he warns of the sweeping koolbardi, even though

The Train to Heidelberg

the only birds we see are pigeons utterly unphased by the people, by the noise, by us. We wear raincoats, but the rain will come later—after three tourists from Perth leave Heidelberg in search of french fries in Ivanhoe.

We are early for our train. My fault. I have a fear of being late, a fear that lateness is the first tile to tumble in a winding line of dominoes. We are always early, loitering at entrances, always lingering in the margins. Today is no different, so we stop at a coffee cart and order double espressos we neither want nor need. I watch him gulp and spill his babyccino, and listen to his plans for more walks, more trains, more trams, more coffees, more profiteroles. All of this is easier than questions about hospitals, MRIs and the brain's failed plans to tell the speech muscles how to move the lips, the jaw, the tongue. So we let him make his plans. These are plans we can keep.

The train to Heidelberg has fifteen stops. Fifteen versions of *are we there yet?* Fifteen requests to push the bell. We read the signs of places we don't know and between my accent and the history of the English language, we invent new quarters, new neighbourhoods, new lives. Little legs swing back and forth without any real rhythm and I complain about the need to use manners and indoor voices in indoor public spaces. But he doesn't complain. He's never once complained of the pain, of the unfairness of it all, of not being able to find his words when he has so much to say, of the paediatrician who says he can't when he does—when he will—of a body that fails and fatigues, of a school holiday not spent on a lark in Melbourne but on a train to Heidelberg to get his brain scanned.

He'll say nothing later either. We'll arrive and he'll put on his adult-sized blue scrubs and pretend to be a doctor. He'll walk through the doors alone with the MRI technicians, lie down on the padded table and watch *Bluey*. Behind the heavy doors we cannot hear his voice—indoor or outdoor—and so we'll wait for time to tick over, not like we're playing at a park killing time, but like we're sitting in the waiting room of a brain centre, hoping that the magnetic fields and radio waves reveal something helpful, but nothing that needs more appointments, more doctors, more trains.

He emerges and asks for a photo in his scrubs. He asks for a snack, a drink of water. He asks which train we'll catch next.

Late to the Party

Jesse Galea

Going to the cinema is an exercise in counting down the minutes until I can leave. My ADHD makes me struggle to sit still and be quiet for the hours it takes to watch a movie, and the lack of subtitles means I'll likely miss half the dialogue anyway. Books are friendlier—able to be put down and picked up at my leisure, not requiring me to sit in a cold, dark room and read the lot in one sitting.

And no offence to my friends, but we have vastly different tastes. If this one is anything like the last dozen we've seen together, the highlight of my night will be the snacks.

But I'm a pushover who likes to feel included, so I eat my popcorn without complaint.

We're in the back row, stretched out over four recliner seats. Beside me are three of my longest-standing friends, some of the only people I still talk to who knew me before I came out the first time around.

The movie starts and I settle into my boredom. I cross my feet over each other, then uncross them.

I wonder if I should've looked up the guy this movie is about before watching it. I'm cautiously confident that he's a musician, but I can't name any of his songs or a single fact about his life. Couldn't tell you if he's still alive.

Onscreen, an orange-clad man storms down a hallway in slow motion. I take a sip of my Coke as the scene jumps back in time to a vibrant musical number during the character's childhood, and maybe I won't hate this as much as I thought I would. My favourite movie is *Ella Enchanted*. I like a good musical number.

My brain tunes out until adult-Reggie is back, singing a song I unexpectedly recognise. I guess I have heard some of his music.

His gaze lingers on a man dancing around him, and I let myself read into the fleeting glance as the music continues and the man disappears into a crowd of dancers. I know I'm overanalysing the scene. I do the same to everything that gives off the slightest suggestion of being anything but cishet, despite (or maybe because of) my adolescence being repeatedly burnt by queerbait.

I've learnt to stop expecting these things to have a payoff, but I let myself indulge in the fantasy.

A musical montage begins, and my feet tap in time with the music.

Before Reggie can climb the steps to a small stage and take his position at the keyboard behind the singers, one of the other musicians stops him. The man gently but urgently pushes him backwards until he's pressed up against the wall and he kisses him and

my
brain
stops.

'Have a good show,' he says as he walks onstage, leaving Reggie—and me—stunned.

I stop thinking, stop blinking, stop breathing.

It's overwhelming. It's 2019. I'm not used to surprise representation.

I went to a Catholic high school whose library was void of characters like me. I'd never read a book with a gay protagonist until earlier this year, and I had to specifically seek it out. It'll be another two years before I read a book with a trans protagonist, and a further six months until I read one written by a trans author.

I sit, electrified and motionless, goosebumps prickling my skin.

For a moment, I'm living in a world that doesn't need to advertise gayness because straightness isn't default. If I want to see myself, I don't need to scour tiny, curated lists for scraps. It's just there.

When the movie finishes, I follow my friends outside, talking with an enthusiasm that I rarely experience, that I hardly know what to do with. *Ella Enchanted* has been officially stripped of its favourite movie status.

'Hang on,' Sophie says, 'you didn't know he was gay before now?'

'No,' I say. 'My parents didn't listen to his music when I was growing up, so I never heard anything about him.'

My friends give me endless shit about it, but I'm grateful for the ignorance that left me overwhelmed and breathless and limitless.

Even if it is baffling that I made it into my twenties without knowing Elton John is gay.

A Non-exhaustive Review of Things that Have Been Yelled at Me from the Window of a Holden Commodore

Alexander Thorpe

- *'Youse dogs are f*cked!'*

This one is elevated above many similar offerings by the use of the plural ('youse dogs'), despite the fact that I was walking alone. At least, I *thought* I was alone. What did this man in his V8 see that I could not? Haunting. **6/10**

- *'Steady on, turbo!'*

Objectively funny. I was struggling to get my bike up Preston Point Road in entirely the wrong gear when a kindly gent overtook me, stopped and shifted into reverse just to deliver this message. Dry, well-timed, not overtly threatening. **8/10**

- *'(Various homophobic slurs)'*

Unoriginal, unhelpful, uninspired. **0/10**

- *'Nice pants! Did you borrow them off your girlfriend?'*

This one was particularly galling as I thought the jeans looked alright on me. And for the record: no, I didn't borrow them. I bought them myself. From Sportsgirl. **5/10**

- *'Oiiiiiiii!'*

What this one lacks in substance, it makes up for in raw, nasal-voweled passion. **6/10**

- *'Get a real horse!'*

Succinct, obscure, sublime. Apparently meaningless, yet carrying the promise of some profound understanding just out of reach. This phrase has worked its way into my head at least once a week for the past fifteen years and will continue to do so for the rest of my life. **10/10**

- *'Marry me!'*

Reader, I did not. **2/10**

The Camp Follower

Carol Mills

From my window seat I can see the angry waves of Bass Strait below. Ahead, a weathered cliff face and, beyond that, emerald-green potato fields. The wind picks up, tossing the aircraft up and down as we begin the final approach into Burnie airport. The pilot warns us to keep our seatbelts tight; it could be a bumpy landing. Just short of the piano keys that signal the start of the runway, the aircraft hits a windshear and lurches wildly.

I grab the seat in front of me as the aircraft banks almost seventy degrees. I can see the ground, the tip of the wing facing downwards, at the wrong angle. A microsecond and the aircraft rights itself, rises slightly, then hits the ground hard before careening down the runway with full flaps. Inside the cabin the overhead lockers shudder and rattle. We slow and stop. The cabin crew announce the arrival and the seatbelt sign is turned off. Silence, no clicking of seatbelts unfastened nor movement of passengers in their seats. Paul stands up, breaking the tension. He grabs his bag from the overhead locker and tells me to get up.

Tomorrow will be Christmas Day, spent in a place I've never been, without family or friends. This trip is one of a series of endless contracts and endless summers. Winters are spent in Queensland where the weather is warm and dry but when the wet season arrives, Paul finds flying work in southern states. It's always exciting, in the beginning. Going to new places, meeting new people. The initial curiosity quickly wanes with the isolation and lack of meaningful contact. It's hard to meet people and make friends when you're only passing through. My only purpose seems to be providing company for Paul. I am the camp follower.

The wind pushes against me as I walk across the tarmac, and I must lean my whole body into it to get inside the terminal building. A junior pilot is waiting to drive us to Strahan on Tasmania's west coast. I'm shivering, so we stop along the road to buy warm socks and a beanie. Two hours later we arrive at the married pilots' accommodation: a donga at the rear of a house shared by two helicopter pilots. The previous occupant was one of the pilot's dogs. He slept on the bed, and while an attempt has been made to clean it up, remnants of dog hair still cling to the mattress.

Paul threatens to leave on the next plane back to Melbourne. I am trying to work out the best option. A clean mattress is located at the chief pilot's house, but he's away and no one has a key. The junior pilot breaks in through a side window. I am handed the clean linen and blankets while the men heave the mattress onto the back of the ute.

The Camp Follower

It snows overnight on Cradle Mountain, a two-hour drive from here. *Well*, Paul says, *it's not summer at least.* We laugh and make the most of it. Tears come later, in phone calls to children. I promise myself, as I always do, that next year will be different.

It takes only ten minutes to walk from the pilots' accommodation to the town centre where the floatplanes are based. Six other pilots work with Paul. Unlike him, they are young and fly for little pay, banking hours for better jobs. Paul is only here to fill the gap while the chief pilot takes a holiday. Occasionally I catch a ride with Paul, flying over the wilderness areas of the west coast. I buy food and cook and wash clothes. I make attempts to embrace my nomadic life.

The contract ends. We head north with a tailwind that makes the flight smooth and uneventful. At home, I make lunch for the family, roast chicken and plum pudding soaked in brandy. I extract the wishbone from the chicken, my pinkie finger holds one end and Paul's the other. I wish for this to be the last of it—the contracts, the Christmases away from home. The bone breaks. It doesn't matter who wins. The next wet season will come and go the same way. I crush the bones and lay them outside in a dish, an offering to the wind.

In Absentia

Jessica Bowker

How are those two little men?
　Six words.
　How often had I heard them over the last eight years? Sometimes taken them for granted. Assumed they'd be asked year after year.
　I'm in the kitchen making dinner when I hear the familiar voice ask the question that has been asked of me so many times, I've lost count. But today, as I stand at the stove watching the bolognese sauce simmer away, the voice sounds more distant. I listen for it again, more intently this time, but nothing. Just the quiet bubbling and popping of the sauce thickening in the pot.
　I feel my heart beginning to race, anxiety building in me like a balloon inflating with each passing second. The smell of boiling tomatoes makes me want to be sick. I turn away from it—try to push the feeling down— reach for my phone lying idle on the kitchen counter. I unlock it with trembling hands and frantically search the voicemail messages. Find the one I am looking for. With last year's date. The one I've saved and keep coming back to. I press the speaker button, turn the volume up and hold the phone to my chest.

In Absentia

I am sucker-punched by the familiar greeting.

Jesse-Jesse.

How my grandmother began all our conversations.

Short for Jessica. Named after her husband, my grandfather Jesse Manfred, who died just three months before I was born. Her first grandchild. She told me I saved her life, that my arrival had tempered her grief and given her something to live for after losing her one true love.

'Yes, Gran,' I hear myself say as I stand alone in the kitchen, the bolognese sauce beginning to burn behind me.

It's just the two of us again. My heart rate begins to slow down as I come to this realisation. The balloon deflates … I exhale … relief floods through me.

How are you, darling?

Her words hang in the air as she pauses to catch her breath.

I want to tell her that I'm okay, taking her advice, trying not to put so much pressure on myself. That I miss our cups of tea and her fluffy scones, her endless wisdom, the way she always listened to me. I want her to tell me about the library books she's been reading. And I want her to know that I'm writing, just as I promised I would.

But the words are trapped, and nothing comes out. Her voice fills the void once more.

And how are those two little men?

I smile at the familiar reference, glad she asked. I want to tell her that Luc is testing and teaching me and that Rhys is surprising me just as she predicted they would. That I love my sons fiercely and yet there are times I don't enjoy being a mother. I want her to reassure me that this is a phase of life, and that it too shall pass. I want to hear her remind me that my children are my number one priority, and while it may be relentless and not always satisfying work, the most important job I have is the one right in front of me.

But she says none of these things, only pauses briefly, clears her throat.

Call me when you can, darling. Bye for now.

I want to scream her back into existence, shout her name until I have no voice left. But there is only silence. End of message. Dinner ruined.

I stand frozen in the kitchen, silent tears streaming down my face, until I am interrupted by the sound of small feet charging down the hallway.

Instinctively, I drop to my knees and open my arms wide. The boys slam into me, almost knocking me off balance, and ripple with laughter. I bury my head into them, feel their breath brushing against my neck, squeezing them tight. My two little men.

All Women

Carmen Cosgrove

We ease in with small talk. The words flow freely as I open my container of leftovers. I set aside thirty minutes for these lunches, but after an hour the words still tumble out and we find it hard to return to our desks.

We sit at a rickety table beneath the safety of a polycarbonate shelter. The weather is warming up again. It feels safer to talk out here, in a courtyard nestled in the valley between two glass-and-concrete office blocks. Inside the building we talk in acronyms and use technical terms. Comfortable topics, compared to the ones we discuss out here.

The first time I had one of these conversations, the two of us rotated around the table following the shade. The last time, the air was fresh but welcome. One small admission about my personal life is met with one of their own. Food is forgotten as we share and listen.

Each story is as different as the person telling it, but the themes remain the same. Two people living in the same house, experiencing two completely different realities. Our stories are intertwined with those of previous generations. His parents. Our parents. Our grandparents.

The women who sit opposite me are ones I've stopped to laugh with when we pass each other in our open-plan office. We've traded compliments on outfits and swapped stories about cheeky children. The men in our lives are rarely mentioned; we don't notice this until one day they are, and we put the conversation on hold until we can meet somewhere more private.

All men are angry and controlling. That is what my mother told me when I called to tell her I was leaving. It was a 39 degree day. I was scuttling back and forth between houses in the five-hour period allotted to me to pack and move.

Today it's my lunch that remains untouched, as I try to make sense of my own story. A story which features the words *safety plan*. How can a phrase with the word safe in it be so terrifying? I was lucky to have a supportive counsellor. We've all been to counselling. As couples. On our own. Some of us are still physically in the family home but have moved on emotionally. Others left several years ago but are still entangled in a web of abuse.

Despite the never-ending stream of women with the same experiences, I don't believe my mother's mantra. I have one of my own. All women are strong and adaptable. My own story has evolved with the weather. The first few times I told it, it was his story. Now it's closer to becoming my own.

The Great Storm

Rochelle Pickles

I've never had another personal encounter quite like it. It was so intimate, then it was over. Sometimes I wonder about him. I didn't even know his name.

I have always referred to it as the Great Storm of Twenty-Ten. Anyone else who was there knows what I'm referring to; no one else who was there calls it that.

I once dated a meteorologist who lamented being posted in Perth because there was 'no weather'. By this he meant—nothing interesting. Perth's weather moves across a sliding scale of perfect: clear and sunny, mildly cloudy, hot, and hot-hot. *It's a dry heat!* we proclaim to every outsider who didn't ask. The meteorologist and his colleagues passed the hours drinking Lipton's and playing Bananagrams. But he wasn't there for the Great Storm of Twenty-Ten.

I was twenty-six and working a telephone respite-service gig at the Australian Red Cross. The calls started coming in not long after lunch, first from our emergency services team, then from friends and family scattered along the storm path. Someone's windows had been smashed in. Flash flooding was cutting off our routes home. It was coming our way, moving down from the north.

The unique thing about the Great Storm was the hailstones. We get very excited about any speck of hail in Perth, on account of the no weather. These hailstones were golf ball–sized and fell with such velocity they smashed windows and dented the roof of every luckless car that happened to be out that day. In the months that followed, those cars could be seen everywhere, top panels dimpled like cellulite. Most were written off, but occasionally you might still come across one today. You'll stop and stare as it cruises by, heart full of nostalgia for the Great Storm.

It was only just beginning to rain at our office in East Perth. If management had left us to clock off at the usual time of 4.30 pm, everything would have been fine. But the Australian Red Cross took these things seriously. We were sent home to safety, at what turned out to be fifteen minutes before the storm passed over the city. I was on the free CAT to the station when the hail started to pummel thunderously against the side of the bus. We moved away from the windows, fearing they'd shatter. The doors opened at Forrest Chase, and I ran through heavy rain to the steps leading up to the overpass.

The Forrest Chase overpass is a small semi-enclosed footbridge that connects the city to the main Perth station, which, at that time, ran four train lines to the farthest reaches of our metro. The bridge is lined by smooth tiles that best serve their purpose on those

The Great Storm

no-weather days. They are, however, slippery when wet. This does not usually pose a problem to a city of calm, slow-walking people, who know to tread carefully on a rainy day. But on *this* day, Perth lost its mind.

Unaccustomed to the excitement and terror of an extreme weather event, we scrambled across the overpass, fearing for our lives and our windows back home.

That's when it happened.

A young man, possibly my age or at least I like to tell myself so, slipped on the tiles and lurched towards me. As a misguided reflex, I moved to raise both my arms, palms up, to catch him. But before my hands had reached high enough for that to have been plausible, and just as he had righted himself enough to no longer be falling, I made full contact with his genitals.

In this young man's attempt to singlehandedly bring back those slinky nylon pants popularised in the late nineties, the fabric between us offered no discernible barrier. I came to know him as only a lover might. Whipping my offending hands back, I mumbled an apology and ran.

I never forgot him, that level of sensory detail impossible to expunge. Does he still think of me too, perhaps every time he crosses the Forrest Chase overpass? No one forgets where they were on the day of the Great Storm.

Ourselves, a Muted Frequency

Sally Thomas

Our writing tutor placed an array of objects on the table. Mementos, photos, letters, silent glimpses into someone else's past. We were archaeologists, spinning stories from our observations. Each object, redefined as a prompt, became the heart of an imagined history.

I had just begun writing when my phone buzzed against the table, dim text declaring a call from my grandmother's nursing home. I slipped out into the hallway. They called twice, thrice, every week, never with good news. At best they would be chasing the payment for her room, the funds still tangled in paperwork, which I worked too slowly to unpick. They otherwise told of scattered injuries: bouts of confusion, falls resulting in small bruises and bumps, reported like little white warning flags. No action to be taken. Just notifications, taps on the shoulder, reminders of her continued decline.

I picked up the call to a muffled argument. The nurse spoke shortly, without introduction. My grandmother was in the lobby and causing a scene, claiming she wanted to go home, that I would pick her up, that she needed to leave now, *now*. An insistence made not from defiance, but desperate confusion. Her mental fugue

Ourselves, a Muted Frequency

had risen slowly in these past months, clinging to the walls like slippery steam and making it hard for her to grasp things once familiar.

The nurse told me to calm her down. I agreed, too quickly, my mind an unwritten map: a compulsion to help, with no plan on how to do so. The phone was handed over. My grandmother's voice wavered, lost and anxious, filled with the panicked resistance of the last sane woman in a world gone mad. She begged me to drive her home. She wanted to get back to her couch, to her television and her afternoon quiz shows, and wrap herself in the blanket of her old routine. These strangers were trying to stop her—why? Hadn't she been here long enough?

I tried to explain, hoping the truth would be more palatable from a familiar voice. I led her through the memories of her admission, only two months ago, of how she had felt unsafe living alone. Her protests quietened but didn't dissipate. She settled into the wounded hush of someone who knows they are being lied to but has lost the fire to protest. I pleaded with her to listen to the staff. Distant, she agreed.

A brief pause as the phone was passed. The nurse chided me for not playing into my grandmother's story: these situations are best settled with a tactful narrative. I should have told her that, yes, I would be there to pick her up, if only she could wait another day. And the same tale the next day, and the next, until she had forgotten the whole affair. I told the nurse I would do so next time, and the line clicked silent.

I stayed in the hallway for a long while. The weariness needed airing; I cracked and cradled my head in my hands. Showing up to the nursing home didn't seem like it would help, but it crossed my mind. There was nothing binding me to the classroom. I could go somewhere, anywhere, away, where the stress could be exhaled without shame. The thought burnt out, never more than an ember. I stayed, in retrospect, for the same reason I kept my friends in the dark.

Her health, her happiness, were my responsibilities, and sinking under the pressures that came with them felt like a personal failing. The dam was permitted to swell, but never to break: each crack, each fault, must be patched as it came, so that no one could see the devastation behind the wall. To see the sadness was to share in it. To spread it meant I had failed.

She would be fine, once the spell had passed. The nurses had it under control. I entered the classroom, as though nothing had happened, and took my seat once more. My friend asked with gentle reassurance, was I alright? I told them that I was. I told myself the same.

That Coat

Annie Horner

There she is again. At the top of the escalator.

'Excuse me. Excuse me,' as I push my way past commuters standing patiently, one behind the other.

At last. I step off the moving stairway and glance left, then right. Yes. There it is. That coat. I know that coat. Tan leather. Fox fur trim at the collar, hem and sleeves.

She walks briskly around the corner leading to the next platform. I quicken my pace. A train pulls out. The platform is empty.

I sit on the bench and breathe deeply. Close my eyes and still my heart. Clear my mind and regain composure.

This is the third time I've seen her. She's always wearing that coat. I've never seen her face. Yet I know her. Somehow, I know her. Her stride. The bounce of her shoulder-length blonde hair. The space she makes in the air around her. Almost an aura.

I'm on the wrong platform for my train so I retrace my steps and get on with my day. I'm visiting old friends in London, friends from almost a lifetime ago. We were Australians abroad in the seventies. Without mortgages or kids, we partied and travelled around Europe. Eventually I returned to the land of sun and sand, but they hunkered down in soggy, grey London. Over the intervening fifty years we've kept in touch and now in our seventies we're reliving the halcyon days—sipping good reds in front of cosy fires. Once again, we are without mortgages or kids, but the pace is almost glacial. It suits us. Naps after lunch. Early nights. Gentle strolls in the great parks of the city.

I hadn't mentioned the woman in the tan coat to my friends. There seemed no point. I hadn't seen her face so maybe I was mistaken in believing I knew her. And yet a few days later there she was again, on an Underground escalator, always headed for the District Line platform. This time I caught up with her.

'Excuse me,' my voice breathy as I reached my hand to her shoulder.

But the sensation was not the cool touch of leather. Instead, I experienced a faint warm breeze as the shoulder dissolved under my hand. She turned and smiled. I stood with my hand outstretched. The next train on the District Line pulled out and the platform was empty.

Of course I knew her. It was me in 1972.

Free of the Earth

Barry Divola

These are the five worst things about being an acrobat in Jemaa el-Fna, the main square in Marrakesh, in ascending order.

1) Car drivers—they don't care if they hit you.
2) Motorbike riders—they *really* don't care if they hit you.
3) Castanet players with twirling fez tassels—they think you're taking away their business.
4) Snake charmers—they think you're taking away their business … *and* they have snakes.
5) The police—they just don't like you.

I'd seen Rahid and Mehdi earlier in the day. They were at a news stand outside the Cafe Argana. Rahid, taller and thinner than his friend, was reading aloud from the newspaper he was holding. Mehdi, stocky and with a wispy shadow of a moustache above his top lip, leaned casually against him. The way he looked at his friend's mouth as it formed the words, rather than scanning the pages himself, suggested that Mehdi didn't know how to read.

An hour later, after I did a slow lap of the square and stopped in a cafe to escape the sun, Rahid went past me.

When I say he went past me, I mean to say he executed one cartwheel, then another, then a backflip, and finally a complicated manoeuvre where he shifted his body sideways through the air, clutched his knees to his chest, and then landed perfectly on his feet, ten metres from where he began.

Mehdi followed with a similar routine, landing a little unsteadily when his left foot, in a grubby imitation Converse sneaker, slipped on a glossy advertising flyer someone had discarded.

They finished their routine with Mehdi leaping up onto Rahid's head, balancing there while they both clapped to attract the attention of those sitting on the open-air balcony of Cafe France.

Then it was time to take off their hats—a Lacoste baseball cap for Rahid; a more traditional canvas cap for Mehdi—and ask for coins with calls of 'merci, merci, merci.'

I gave them the loose coins in my pocket, and they let me follow them from Cafe France to Cafe Argana, Cafe Glacier, and then two separate displays at the sprawling Cafe Toubkai. They took a short break to sit in the middle of the square, catch some breath, drink some water, and then it was off for another round.

Seven days a week, 10 am to 2 pm. One hundred to 150 dirham each for their trouble, as long as the police didn't arrive to move them on for annoying the tourists sipping their mint tea and flicking through photos on their phones.

At least the tourists gave better tips. The locals may cough up a dirham here, a dirham there, but tourists threw five or ten their way, or even a euro or a US dollar if God was smiling that day.

Rahid, who was born in Marrakesh, spoke halting English.

Mehdi, who was from Berber stock in the Atlas Mountains, spoke none.

I asked Rahid what he liked about being an acrobat, or as he called it, a tumbler.

'It is good for body,' he said, after thinking for a moment. 'I am with my friend, and we make money in a good way, not in a bad way.'

Mehdi touched his friend's arm and asked him something in Arabic. Rahid answered him, and then Mehdi responded.

'He asks me what you ask,' Rahid said to me. 'I told him you asked what we like about being a tumbler. He said he likes it because he is free of the earth for a small time. You understand?'

I looked at both of them, sitting on the dirty ground amid the snake charmers, the castanet players, the fortune tellers and the spruikers of Jemaa el-Fna.

'Yes,' I said. 'I understand.'

Six months later I read the news. A bomb had rocked Jemaa el-Fna. The blast tore apart Cafe Argana.

It was the cafe where I had first seen Rahid and Mehdi. It was on their regular route.

They worked from 10 am until 2 pm. The blast occurred just before noon.

I read further. Seventeen killed; many more injured.

Were they in that number? Were they free of the earth?

I don't believe in God, or Mohammed, or Allah. But I sent up a prayer anyway, to whoever might be listening.

The Nit Note

Zoe Deleuil

Our morning walks to Kita were long, with foot dragging and bakery bribes, and we were often the last to arrive. One day, a sign went up on the noticeboard that I sensed was addressed directly to me and was not—despite the lavish application of love hearts and flowery lettering—altogether friendly.

Damit wir gemütlich und ruhig in den Tag starten können würden wir uns wünschen, das alle Kinder bis spätsestens 8.50 h in der Kita sind.

I took a photo of it on my phone and then went home to translate it.

For a comfortable and calm start to the day we wish for all children to be at the Kita by 8.50 am at the latest.

The next day we were, as usual, running late. Unable to face the sign, I gave Rafa a day off and we went to the zoo, where we saw white wolves and snowdrops, or *Schneeglockchen*, pushing through the carpet of brown oak leaves and veined ivy. Spring was getting closer; soon this first German winter would be over. In the playground the shadows were long, the trees covered in early white blossom. Rafa ordered me to watch his every move: scaling a wooden house with an orange rope, swinging along the monkey bars, bouncing on a black rubber trampoline, stepping along a green wall with cut-outs for his feet. He looked back at me frequently with a smile, as if checking that I was still there. And then he drew a love heart in the grey playground sand and gazed up at me.

A few days later, a new sign went up in the Kita. This one was handwritten in an extravagant pink pen, with an ominous flurry of exclamation marks dotted with hearts instead of circles. I approached it with trepidation and read it slowly, absorbing the key message.

Liebe Mamas, liebe Papas!
Strassenschuhe, das ist klar,
Sind für Strassen wunderbar!
In den Gruppenräumen, oh nein,
Da gehörn sie nicht hinein!

Shoes, for the street, are wonderful. In the group room, no, was the jist of it. Along with the last line: *they don't belong here.* The *Sie*, in this final sentence, meant *they*, but it could also mean *she*. And I knew, without a doubt, that it had been pinned up with me, the witless *Mutter von Australien* and her muddy boots in mind. The staff member *und die Kinder* were its signatories. My face, already hot in the overheated fug of the hallway, flushed even more. Of course, I should have known not to walk

The Nit Note

into the kids' room with my boots on. But why didn't she just tell me, weeks ago?

Another Monday morning. Weak, cold sun and, for the first time in months, birdsong.

'Rafa!' I said, 'The birds are back. Telling each other about their holidays.'

We rang the doorbell to the Kita and arrived in the dressing room on time, with lots of other kids struggling out of their boots and mittens and putting on their house shoes. Down the hallway wafted the smell of lunch cooking, a mix of soupy vegetables and stewed meat. On the noticeboard was a brand new sign. After a steady, deep inhalation, as I'd been taught in a long-ago mindfulness class, I approached it.

Wir haben Lauser in die Kita.

I felt a strange mix of emotions when I read this note. A quiet pride, because I could read and understand every word, and didn't need to photograph the note and translate it back at home. But also, a familiar dread. Of course, I thought. Of course it would be the sodding Nit Note that transcended cultural and geographical borders. And I really didn't need to be dealing with *Lauser* on top of everything else.

For a moment, remembering former nit infestations in Australia, I panicked. Had we unknowingly imported Australian nits, which had mated with their German counterparts and created a super-resistant *Uber-Nit*?

But these nits could not be pinned on me. We'd been here too long. And the kids hadn't been scratching their heads. So I relaxed, and carried the phrase home with me, repeating it to myself through the day.

Wir haben Lauser in die Kita. My first full German sentence.

Racing Heart

Tess Allen

It's unseasonably hot for a Copenhagen spring day. A bead of sweat trickles down my temple. My bent arms move like pistons, powering me. Somewhere, he's here too. Behind me? Ahead? Every now and then I find myself glancing around but, so far, there's no sight of him. Since the starter pistol fired, I've let the surge of other runners, eager to race, take me away.

I've lost count of the miles. The finish line feels so far away. Endless crowds line the streets behind metal barricades. A sea of red and white flags—the Danish cross—wave either side of me. There's an excitement in the air. I hear it in the music. I see it on the faces of the crowd. But I'm separate from it all. Alone in my sorrow-filled bubble. I will my feet to move to the beat. An attempt to distract myself from the cacophony of thoughts that swirl like a maelstrom.

I see his face. As if it's yesterday all over again. His words hit me like fresh blows. After five years, we're done. The life we had built together dissipating. Afterwards, his blue eyes had turned away as I'd gazed through the moving bus window. As if I'd broken his heart, not the other way around. We had trained together. Been friends, lovers, everything. Now, I was alone.

'Can't we just run this one together?' he'd said, having found me, dazed from lack of sleep, at the start line. A last goodbye. Tears had welled as I'd turned away.

My tongue peels itself from the roof of my mouth, finding its way to a sweat bead resting precariously on my lip. Behind suncream-smeared sunnies, I welcome the sight of a drink station ahead. Red cups are lined up in rows on the table, like soldiers awaiting deployment. I slow my steps, not daring to stop. Reaching out my hand, someone passes me a cup. Returning to the road, I gulp the cool water down. Replenishing spent tears.

A giant red signpost signals, in large white letters, 25 miles. One to go. I wiggle my fingers. They're like sausages, squishy and swollen. The skin of my inner thighs burns, chaffed from hours of friction. My feet, my head, my heart—everything hurts. I can't do this. I'm not good enough. Not good enough for him. I feel my steps slow as I glance over my shoulder. To my left, a couple of runners behind. Was that his green Nike shirt? I check again. His blue runners? My heart leaps into my throat. Sadness and anger well inside like a swollen river, threatening to burst its banks.

I grit my teeth. Around me, I hear the grunts and panting of fellow runners. We're all in pain, just in different ways. A sea of onlookers yell, clap and cheer. An indiscernible jumble of sounds. I can do this. I pick up speed, one foot in front of the other towards the

Racing Heart

finish. Nails dig into palms as I clench my fists. It's as though I no longer have control of my legs. I make my way along the water's edge, a hint of salty air wafting across my path.

The red banner drapes above the road like a giant sash. On the approach, people jump and scream. They don't know me, and I don't know them. But, in this moment, it doesn't matter.

I cross the line. 42.1 kilometres. 26.2 miles. A grinning woman approaches, handing me water and placing a finisher medal around my neck. The cool metal rests against my chest. I lift my hands, covering my face as fresh tears come. I move through the crowd and sit on the soft grass, legs outstretched, sipping water as I watch other finishers come in. He's not among them.

Then, from the corner of my eye, I see those familiar blue runners. That familiar green shirt. The matching green cap. I take a deep breath as I stand, legs wobbling. I approach him as he kneels on the ground. He who broke my heart. I tap him on the shoulder, and he looks up. It's not him. He's nowhere to be seen. I apologise to the stranger, my cheeks already reddened by the heat. I clutch my medal and smile as I walk away.

Jasmine and Nostalgia

Sarah Moredoundt

There is a tiny hint of jasmine in the air and with it comes dreams of a summer just about to fruit. I have woken early to a mess of five-year-old boy limbs across my belly; my own legs cramped in the single bed I am sharing with my youngest born and our giant, heavy pup who thinks he is my third child. Flynn's warm breath is on my cheek as I listen to my oldest asleep above us, master of the bunk beds. Elliot is experiencing hay fever for the first time, so his usually silent night breathing is snuffly and deep. He suddenly laughs loudly—deep and different to when he is awake. I wonder when my eight-year-old slipped from young boy to pre-teen without me noticing. I smile as I imagine what hilarity he is sharing with his mates while dreaming.

In a handful of minutes, the alarm will sound, and we will begin the whirlwind that is getting to school and work. Will Elliot remain patient with his furiously bossy little brother? Will Flynn insist on me creating magnet block creations for 'just one more minute!' as I juggle breakfast and school lunches, packing overnight bags for my darling babes' second home at their dad's? Will the boys be on top of each other, wrestling and laughing

Jasmine and Nostalgia

with gusto as only young boys can, until inevitably someone hits too hard, a pillow in the nose and then a stream of cherry-red blood, tissues, and watery eyes but still mostly happy smiles? Especially when Elliot, the mediator and comedian, makes a penis joke to cheer up Flynn, the warrior and wildling.

I think of this as I feel the warm feet pressing into my skin, marvelling that not so long ago I was growing those very feet and now they are attached to a very tall and lanky baby man. I savour these minutes, weary in my bones but full beyond measure in my heart. I picture our summer—mornings at Little Athletics, long beach days blasting 'Watermelon Sugar' and sucking on icy poles, bike rides and king of the hill, and bushwalks with Sunny, our German shorthaired pointer (who is completely mad but as Elliot likes to say, so are we). Then the quiet nights together on the couch—sun-kissed and soaked in salt and love.

I close my eyes and smell the tiny hint of jasmine. I wish for nothing but this right here, this perfect, simple moment just for us.

Sighted Swallow Swarm

Tiffany Hastie

A small coastal town, swallowing down new residents in fistfuls. New suburbs of ticky-tack homes with touching rooftops, compensating for lack of yards with poked-in green spaces. Winding rabbit warrens of streets where sheep paddocks used to be, and before that, bush.

I had watched the town grow, watched it expand along with my own belly, and as I drove my boys down the river road that day, the birds came. Thousands of tiny swallows, small and brown and insignificant but for their vast number. Filling the skies with caterwauls and spins, dropping and twirling on a breeze too light to feel. And on the road, their bodies.

The first day we stopped. Scooped up the tiny shivering body, heart thudding under thin feathered chest, tiny claws gripping at my thick-skinned palms. Balled it up in a jumper on the front seat. It was dead by the time I walked the kids to class. I stopped on the river road where I'd picked it up and shuffled it out, there on the riverbank, amongst its fallen comrades, and went home to wash the jumper.

It wasn't a morning thing, it wasn't the last dancing flight before dusk, it was always. Spinning and

Sighted Swallow Swarm

circling, like orcas bubble hunting, encircling prey and pouncing—only there was no prey. The birds just flew in every direction at once, their bodies littering the bitumen. Unavoidable.

The birds filling the sky like falling stars was not the weirdest thing for those three weeks. The weirdest thing was that no one was surprised.

Pulled over to the side of the road I marvelled, mouth open as wide as my car door as they dived again and again into the cars. Like a fog that wouldn't clear. The weirdest thing was that when I questioned the display, the suicidal swarming that had descended, the locals said it happened every year. Nothing unusual.

But I was local. I had been raised on a farm twenty k's out of town, I'd caught the orange bus in with the other rural kids, I'd worked at the first Maccas when it opened, I remembered when both the primary school and the hardware store were in the main street of town—where the two-storey cinema, with Timezone and Dôme below it, now stood. My nan had broken her nose tripping over the uneven pavement walking down Prince Street to get her scratchies. I'd broken my wrist bonnet-surfing down the main street at fourteen. I'd been left pregnant twice here. Yet I had no memory of this ever happening before.

No one reported the swarm in the news. No one likened it to Hitchcock's *The Birds*. They all just got on with life, driving through the swarm, stepping over the twitching bodies littering the sidewalk. The tiny brown birds were seen like insects, so many in the air above that those on the ground could be ignored. But seeing the small, feathered splatters dotting the roads, mashed further into the grain with every wheel, was hard for me. My sons felt it too.

The swarm favoured the point where the river wound closest to the town centre. Maybe they had come there before, drawn by flying ants or mosquito swarming when this was all wetlands. Maybe our town had spread quicker than they could evolve flight patterns.

But still, I had never seen this before.

And I haven't seen it since. Never, since that year over a decade ago, have the birds swarmed the town. The uncanny valley of it lives in my mind because no one else remembers. When I talk about the year the birds swarmed, they look at me with quirked brow, 'You mean spring?'

'No,' I say. 'The year the birds came. All those tiny brown birds that spent themselves against our windshields and cars and littered the sky.'

'Oh,' they say, 'I don't remember that.'

Where Does All that Sorrow Go?

Aksel Dadswell

Road rage and roadworks and the flesh of roadkill, scattered in bright sorrowful gobbets across the highway, mark my drive to work every morning from Busselton to Bunbury.

There's more roadkill than ever lately, the wildlife disturbed by the culling of trees and carving of land that's part of the Bunbury Outer Ring Road, a years-long construction that's all about creating safer conditions for drivers, our wheels clotted with bits of obliterated fauna.

I pass a dead kangaroo on my way through the Ludlow Tuart Forest, the bloat and collapse and decay of its corpse marking the passage of time for a commute that otherwise blurs into a meaningless smear. When the roo's bones show through, I wonder if its ghost will haunt the landscape, and how many other ghosts dwell there.

Turning off the tuart drive onto the highway, a pair of smokestacks, their tips striped red and white like candy canes, poke their heads above the horizon of trees. Clouds, brighter and whiter than the real thing, spew from their mouths into the brittle blue of the late winter sky.

I don't know what kind of factory they belong to. I could follow the road to its destination or do some research, but I won't. What they belong to doesn't matter as much as the story I've attached to them.

I remember seeing these smokestacks as a kid whenever we went on a car trip. They'd dip in and out of sight as we drove, and I'd twist myself about in the car to catch a glimpse of them and the bright shapes they emitted. I could never see more than the smokestacks, and I was burning to know what they were attached to.

I asked Mum what they were, and she explained they were basically giant chimneys for a factory. I knew factories were big buildings where all sorts of things were made by machines performing repetitive tasks and people standing at conveyer belts, and I asked what this factory made. Mum hesitated, and then she told me, in that low, breathless tone she saved for the most exciting bits of knowledge, that it was a cloud factory. Those white shapes emerging from the chimneys were its product. Not chocolate or toys or toasters or cars. Clouds.

I was obsessed, and overflowing with incessant questions, all deftly parried by Mum. What are clouds made of? What ingredients are put into them? How many clouds does it take to fill up the sky? How long do they last? Do they have different factories for storm clouds and happy clouds?

Mum was always adept at telling stories, and even better at making them up on the spot in response to the kind of questions you only get from annoyingly curious kids with no understanding of the world. I remember her telling me that they were made from the emotions of everyone who lived in the area. That's why we have seasons, to show that different emotions aren't bad but part of a natural cycle. That's why it's important to appreciate and accept gloomy, rainy days, because that's everyone's sorrow coming down on us, and rather than making us sadder or getting us down we know that everybody else feels the same way sometimes, and the rain and the dark can show us that we don't have to feel so alone.

I love that story, and every time it rains I think of all the sorrow and pain in the world. I also think about the smokestacks as I drive past the machinery and the mountains of woodchips that used to be trees, and the bare stretches of dirt soon to be road. I think about the way Mum hesitated when I asked about the factory, and the stories we tell children to avoid the truth, or to cover for something we can't, or don't yet want to, explain. We think kids can't process the harsher realities of the world, so we make up stories instead.

Traffic slows up ahead. A fox lies in a ruin of fur and bright open meat in the middle of the road.

I feel sick and sad for the anonymous losses spanning the length of this road and beyond. I wonder what happens when all that rain made from everybody's sorrow falls to earth, soaking into the soil and feeding the plants and flooding the rivers.

Cars swerve to avoid the fox, skirting its ruin, leaving the clean-up for someone else.

A Man in a Van

Ros Thomas

We are gunning towards Kalgoorlie on a week-long road trip. My beloved is enthroned in the driver's seat of our hired motor home. Two out of three teenagers are strapped in the back, squabbling over a box of Jatz crackers. I've eaten an entire packet of Twisties in the sixteen minutes between Meckering and Cunderdin.

I am yet to meet a man who can resist the call of the open road. Mine croons the backing vocals to 'Slip Slidin' Away', then launches into a falsetto for the chorus.

A road train roars past, buffeting us sideways. I catch a glimpse of the Hulk Hogan in charge and the sign on his dash: 'Highway Warrior'.

'Wouldn't want to get on the wrong side of him,' I say.

'Yup. We're a special breed,' replies my soft-skinned accountant, caressing the plastic wheel of his white Jayco Conquest. 'Drive into the sunset, rise with the dawn.'

He settles smugly into his seat as I shift uncomfortably in mine, silently begging for an interruption to the treeless view. An unbroken ribbon of grey highway vanishes over the horizon. I study the mallee scrub for signs of life, but it refuses to offer up even a crow. I'm momentarily absorbed by a dark lump on the roadside up ahead. Could it be a goanna? As we bear down on it, I realise it's only a jagged strip of tyre.

'Road alligators,' mutters the wannabe truckie, elbowing his pale arm out the driver's side window. I note the succession of coffee drips staining the front of his polo. His left leg—rendered useless by cruise control—flops in the footwell. A camel-brown ugg boot ensures against holiday frostbite. He wears a roomy pair of elasticated trousers to keep himself nice.

A speck appears on the horizon: bigger than a car, smaller than a road train. It grows a high roof cab, a boxy body and becomes a shimmering mirage of white. It's another Jayco Conquest. As we close the gap, my driver slides one hand to the top of the steering wheel and casually extends his index finger in a passing salute. The other driver reciprocates as he zooms past.

'The brotherhood of the road is alive and well,' says my husband with a satisfied sigh.

The next four hours of driving stretch eastwards with barely a bend in the road. I force the sulks in the back to say sorry for the mean, hurtful, accurate things they said to each other. After Burracoppin, the salmon gums return, shading the highway with their green parachute canopies. By Bodallin, a flotilla of flat-bottomed clouds has gathered on the horizon.

Periodically, my Wheatbelt tour guide gestures vaguely towards some feature of the landscape requiring my attention.

'Sheep?' I offer, having no clue what he's pointing at.

'Wheat silo,' he says flatly, after I've missed it. Minutes later, he signals towards the window again.

'Shed?' I attempt, as we whizz past a humpy of rusted tin.

'Windmill,' he corrects.

I give up and examine the gnat flapping frantically against the windscreen. I marvel at its staying power, four tiny wings a blur of desperation. And then I twig. It's our slipstream that's powering those wings. The gnat's splattered innards have glued his body to the glass. He's probably been dead since Walgoolan. I while away the next hour classifying the streaks and smears dotting the windshield. After identifying one wasp and a cicada, I lose interest. I practice my powers of perception instead, using each insect splodge as a Rorschach test. In the dark stain of a flattened mosquito, I see the delicate wings of a miniaturised butterfly. Who knew bug juice could give such artistic pleasure?

We pass through Southern Cross as the sun dips behind us. The last shafts of daylight drench the cab in golden light, giving my husband the tan he always wanted. His left nostril is aglow. The setting sun turns the thicket of hair on his forearm the colour of beer. The monotony of the darkening highway is broken by another motor home barrelling towards us. My husband delivers his customary one-finger salute but the van's grey-haired occupants stare stonily ahead. They pass us without acknowledgment.

A Man in a Van

'They didn't wave at you, honey,' I say, feeling miffed on his behalf. 'How dare they ignore the brotherhood of the road?'

'Foreigners,' he says. 'Any Twisties left?'

Stuck

Angel Hayward

On my way home from work, where the lights are fluorescent and harsh and the tasks are never-ending, I swing by the liquor store and grab a bottle of wine. It's a night like others spent sitting on the couch, drinking a glass of wine and eating whatever I can order on my phone.

This night, I watch *Dead Poet's Society* and there's a scene where Robin Williams encourages everyone to carpe diem and to suck on the marrow of life. The scene reminds me that there is more to life than working in an office, buying a house, getting married, having 2.5 kids and then retiring.

I need to stop and listen to the wild within me. I need to throw open the door of my prison of expectation and responsibility, fly away and eat street food from around the world, experience different landscapes and meet people from different cultures.

This night, I look into the mirror but don't recognise the reflection.

Viewfinder

Em Readman

I'm on the verge of running late. I'm standing in front of the only full-length mirror in the house. It needs to be cleaned, with specks and fingerprints littering the glass. I stand there in the half-light; the place is not quite dark enough to turn on the lamps, so the walls bruise purple while the sun sets. There is condensation on the windows. My body clutches the shadows.

The scars on my chest are starting to heal, the weeks rolling by and carrying away more swelling with them. They're a reminder of tissue taken, something else gained in its place. I try on another shirt, fumbling with the buttons. I take it off. I pull another on, draping it over my new body, then take it off again. It is difficult to pick the right thing to wear, to find what feels right. My friend Clem once gave me advice for gender-affirming clothing choices.

'Wear boxers with feminine clothing, lingerie with masculine clothing.'

It's good advice, but tough to follow when a pile of clothes are growing at my ankles. I watch my body's reflection keenly. I am seeing it as a body not a wound for the first time in weeks, not a stranger for the first time in my life. Despite it being time to go, I cannot stop looking.

My shoulders do not slope forward anymore, no longer hunched from a mix of heaviness and shame. My torso is longer than I thought it was. Despite a gruelling healing process after the operation, my skin has remained soft around the scarring. My heart is now closer to my skin's surface, and when I lie on my stomach I can feel it beating against the mattress. Before, I wouldn't get dressed in front of a mirror, let alone take it this slowly. Running my eyes over my body, I trail my hands over my skin. A feeling of disgust does not follow. Before, my body felt like a vessel moulded from wet clay. I was unformed, unfinished.

I start hunting around the room. Opening drawers, rifling through bags, picking apart shelves. I am looking for my camera. I haven't used it in years, much less taken a picture of myself. I've rarely felt the desire to chronicle my body below the collarbone, hoping to forget about it, at least for a moment. The absence of that discomfort is so novel. I feel compelled to memorialise this. There are pictures of me in the mirror over the years, nestled in a folder on my phone titled 'before'. Each time I took one I had the goal in mind of casting off my old self, hoping to meet a new person the next time I came to the mirror. I think this may be my first 'after' photo.

The camera is under the bed, viewfinder dusty. I hold it up to my face and watch my body in the mirror through the little window. Soft hips, broad shoulders,

Viewfinder

chest flat at last. I am just that, a body in a mirror, a body I recognise to be mine. I feel affirmed, reconciled. I have come home to my body. There's just enough light left to take the picture.

Escapisms

Coral Montero Lopez

When I was seven years old, I used to pack my dad's old gym bag with all my favourite toys and clothes. I would then announce to my mother that I was leaving home, go outside and sit in front of the car. Sitting there alone and fearful, I wanted to escape my young life, as I could sense my parents' relationship fracturing and didn't want to be a witness anymore. But above all, I was excited to go out and explore the world.

When people ask me where I come from, I tell them that I am from that part of the world where magic casually cohabits with reality. Where I was born in Mexico, no one bats an eyelid if spirits roam freely inside a house, or ghosts wander through town because they don't know they are dead yet. I grew up believing that 'punishing' San Antonio (St Anthony) by turning his image upside down would help a spinster aunty find a boyfriend. Or, if you were a mischievous child, there was a crying lady, La Llorona, who would come and steal you to replace her own children who she killed in a spurt of craziness. Death, in my culture, has a continuous presence; we dance with her, sleep with our departed in the cemeteries, and yet no child is afraid.

Escapisms

I know now that many of those stories were made up. Magical narratives to keep the sacred order in our lives. But there were also the real escapes, by our forefathers who had to provide for their families during the Revolution. In small towns, mothers boiled legumes and grey vegetables to feed their children. When the vegetables became scarce, they boiled old rags that their children would eat mixed with black beans. Those rags were most likely from the clothes of deceased people, but no one flinched. This was the only way many escaped a tragic end.

My maternal grandparents had twenty-one children, and from those, only sixteen are still alive today. When I was little, my cousins and I would challenge each other to say all our aunts and uncles' names in chronological order. From an early age, older children oversaw the younger ones, raising two or three younger siblings while watching helplessly as their mother gave birth to more babies year after year. Learning my mother's place in that ladder made me understand why she had to escape her family so young, only to end up in another household that she would eventually feel the urge to run away from.

I left my old life behind too. I ended up coming to this land, also full of stories older than time. On the outside I was putting behind an infructuous marriage, but it was that urge to explore the world that returned to me, with even more intensity than when I was a young girl. It's funny how I needed to travel to the other side of the world to finally stop running away, to stop escaping from myself. I found my place in this ancient landscape, so different to my homeland, and yet so similar, full of stories that I instinctively understood. I saw the spirits and understood them, even though nobody taught me their words. Perhaps all spirits speak a universal language, a type of ghostly Esperanto, and only those who grew up listening to their songs can attune themselves to it.

I don't run away from anything, and certainly not from myself anymore. I let the spirits talk to me, while I admire the life I've built here. I see new roots grow from my torn arms, seeking earth for grounding. It may be the end of a long saga of escapes in my life history. But the urge to escape is always there, lingering, whispering in my ear.

My Sister, the Mythical Creature

Ellie Cottrell

We were in the car when Mum told us. 'Did you kids know you have a half-sister?' I remember her saying it with a kind of measured nonchalance, no doubt trying to make the words land with a softer thud. I was eleven years old, the big sister—the biggest sister, I'd always thought.

My main recollection of the moment is how sick I felt. For the first time 'the room swam' made sense to me—although nothing about the rest of it did. I was the oldest of four, then suddenly … I wasn't.

I don't recall my siblings being affected in the same way I was. Perhaps they were just too young to understand? Our dad had fathered a child with another woman. A woman who wasn't our mother. Before I was born.

I found out later that Mum chose to tell us then because her friend had urged her to. Her friend who we'd just visited. I respect that now, because it's the kind of thing I do too: make a decision and then act on it immediately. And while I believe Mum came to regret it, I am glad she told us. Because, well, it was either that or never knowing. Never knowing that somewhere out there, a stranger shares my blood.

I have a half-sister, but she's no more real to me than a mythical creature—a unicorn, a dragon. We've never met. I know she got married and I'm pretty sure she has kids. God, it's weird to think I'm an aunt.

The information about her stopped filtering through a long time ago.

We've never met, because—simply put—she doesn't want to know us. We did come close once. It wasn't long after I found out about her existence.

Dad had taken me to see a local production of *Les Misérables*. I was fresh off my own theatre experience, having just played Annie in my school musical—so this was VERY. EXCITING. Not to mention that being from a big family, we rarely got one-on-one time with our parents. I loved every second of that musical, holding back tears during all the sad bits and imagining myself under the spotlight, singing 'On My Own.'

Towards the end, dad leaned over to me and whispered, 'What do you think of Madame Thénardier?'

'She's really good!' I enthused, meaning it. The actress playing her was fizzing with energy and had *great* comedic timing.

'She's your sister,' he replied, almost conspiratorially.

Again, the room swam. How does the quote go? 'We do the best we can with what we know at the time', or something like that. I love my parents fiercely, and I truly believe they were doing the best they could at the time.

My Sister, the Mythical Creature

When the show ended, I asked Dad if my sister knew I was there. Yes, she knew. I asked if I could meet her. He was confident I could, asking me to wait just a moment as he went backstage to check. He was gone for longer than I thought he would be, and the dejected look on his face when he returned was all the answer I needed.

How could he possibly explain it to a child? 'You'll meet her another time,' he reassured me.

Neither of us knew then that this was a lie.

Eleven times three is thirty-three, the age I am now. I can see it from her point of view these days. She came along before my dad even met my mum—the woman he made a family with. I can imagine the hurt. I can imagine the middle-finger 'fuck you' feeling, even if that's not how it was.

Eleven times three is thirty-three, but with all the nuance those numbers bring, I do nurse a tiny wound for the little girl who—just for a moment—looked up to a big sister. A big sister who loved to sing and make people laugh. Am I still that little girl, deep down? Sometimes I feel like it. Sometimes I'm even back there—sitting in the audience with a pounding heart, patiently waiting to meet her.

Pain(t)

Amber Moffat

They say you can't remember anything from being a baby, but I remember this: *Brown paint sliding over an undulating surface. Rich and glossy, there's a hint of fox-red in the brown. A pulsing beneath mud.* I didn't have these words as a baby, of course. They are what I dig from the image now. But I want you to know I was enchanted by this slick of russet. Delighted by its quickness, the way it gleamed with tiny licks of light. Then, *fire in my skin. Sudden and intense. My body roars, bucks against the burn. Nothing but pain.*

I tell my mother about this memory, many years later. She says my father was painting the corrugated iron fence that separated our backyard from the neighbour's. My father held me on his hip as he painted. I was naked except for a nappy, my plump eight-month-old limbs enjoying their first summer. Then, the terrible shriek of a baby in pain. Panicked, they checked my whole body, found redness on my leg. A rag soaked in mineral turpentine had been hooked into the belt of my father's jeans. I had a chemical burn.

The brown fence is a constant of my childhood. I hate its shade of brown, the same colour as the vinyl arms of

Pain(t)

the hand-me-down couch we got from my grandparents. The same brown that often gets paired with orange, screaming 1970s. I'm a child of the 80s. I like pastels, hot-pink and turquoise. But I am drawn to the brown fence because of what lies beyond it.

Our neighbour is a large man, old and angry. His wife is dead. Mum says he is Catholic and he used to beat his wife. I don't understand what either of these things mean, but I'm scared when I hear the slow thud of his steps. Sometimes, when I'm sure the neighbour's not there, I climb onto the coal bin and peer into his backyard. Under my hands, the brown paint is flaky, dry.

The first person I know who goes to art school is the neighbour's grand-daughter. She and her daughter come to live next door when I'm fifteen. She has a pierced nose, Doc Marten boots, op-shop clothes. Sometimes she talks nonstop, rambling stories about sex, drugs and art. Sometimes she lies in bed for days, and her daughter comes to stay at our place. They house-sit for us while we attend a family wedding and when we get home, our kitchen bench is covered in dirty cat-food cans. Each can crawling with fat white maggots.

I recently found a painting I made as a young child. It's a black creature, mouth open, huge eye. It's my childhood cat, Mountain. He's painted with a thick brush, each body part a single stroke. In his middle there's a smear of red paint slashed over a dab of white—an abscess. Mountain often fought with neighbourhood cats, their yowls twisting the night air, erratic and terrifying. His wounds fascinated me. Stickiness, pain, the drama of the body. Looking at this painting now, I think it's the best piece of art I'll ever make.

I didn't plan to major in painting at art school. It felt like a waste. Other majors gave you access to specialist facilities. Dark rooms, kilns, bandsaws. But I couldn't resist painting. The animal-twitch of the brush. Building a world from layers, choosing what to paint over, what to reveal. I'm still gripped by colour slipping over surface. Because paint is most potent when wet. And pain, bold painter of memory, always there.

Holy Family

Will Yeoman

I pull the wool over my eyes. It's the early 80s and I'm deep in a fleecy cloud, hoping to have a quick kip before afternoon smoko ends and it's back to the skirting table. The cocky and his dogs are with the mob, the team's, well, smoking, but also listening to dad playing a *solea* on my guitar, the son of a bitch is pretty damn good too, some Paco de Lucia *falsetas*, some of his own invention, all expertly, soulfully executed (can a Scotsman feel *duende*?) and a lighting *alzapua*. The other rouseabouts and shearers look like they're witnessing a miracle.

    I can't sleep. Instead, I think of Mum, back home, busy keeping out of the sun because she believes the faintest tan will give her skin enough extra colour to out her as mixed heritage once and for all. I think she's beautiful, looks a lot like the Virgin Mary in that Botticelli *tondo*—Mum and me, we're Catholic, so the Marian comparison—but with a lovely Polynesian complexion. Yet she's ashamed of her Samoan culture. I remember the time her sister came from Apia to stay with us. One night Mum and Dad had visitors over for dinner. 'I want you both to go to your room and don't come out until they're gone,' says Mum. Not to us kids but to her sister and my nan on my father's side—the nan who always lived with us because she was sick of always taking a hiding from her drunken prick of a husband, the nan who many years later would suffer a stroke and be scooped up by my full-on god-bothering brother, that strange angel, and placed tenderly on her bed only to refuse a doctor and die hours later, atheist and unrepentant—anyway, as my aunt's preparing to go home after a week of my mum ignoring her, she's crying and hugging me and saying, '*Aue*, when will your mother come back to her people?' My mum's son, I'm just embarrassed.

I look over to my father, still showing off his flamenco chops. Dad—also an atheist—never seemed to care one way or the other about Mum's racial makeup. If anything, he probably found her 'exotic' when they first met in New Zealand. Unfortunately, he inherited his father's taste for the grog, so things turned sour pretty quickly. That's why Dad loves being away from home. But not me. I want my cot in the renovated sleepout on the other side of our carport, surrounded by my guitars and Airfix models and Olivia Newton John posters and the crucifix Sister Anne gave me on my confirmation. Better than this hot shed with its dust and sheep shit and dirty wool greasy with lanolin. Then again, piling up the rolled fleeces, day in day out, ready for being pressed into bales, I guess I make this bed. So I should sleep in it.

Share House Story

Sharron Booth

A tall, slim girl with long blonde hair floated out of the bathroom and smiled. 'Hi, I'm Ariel. Sorry, the phone fell under the bed and we didn't know where it was.'

She meant the alarm that pierced our Sunday morning at seven. My boyfriend of several months had leapt out of bed, swearing, to investigate the noise.

Could someone my age have a boyfriend?

I'd heard him open the door … voices … a door closing, then the stubble and warmth of him under the doona.

'I just walked in on my son and a young lady,' he'd said. 'Josh was out cold, but she woke up.'

'He'll be angry about that.'

'I wonder if it's a casual hook-up or if he's been seeing her for a while?'

'You can't ask. Josh is an adult.'

'And one of his mates is crashed out on the couch.'

His son. A girl. A mate. His daughter Emily asleep in her room after a late shift at McDonald's. And me, old enough to be their mother. A full house.

Ariel wore a pink triangle top and denim mini. She rubbed under her eye—a smudge of last night's mascara, dark circles, or both. She looked fresh-faced and completely trashed at the same time; the perfect Venn diagram of a woman in her early twenties.

'Really sorry!' Ariel held the bathroom door open for me.

Good skin, good teeth, good manners. She rubbed her other eye, and I wondered if she'd slept with contact lenses in. I almost said, 'Ariel, there's a bottle of Opti-Free and some cleanser and moisturiser on the bottom shelf, it's only pharmacy brand but help yourself to whatever you like.' Ariel seemed so self-assured, not to mention clean-skinned, that I realised she must have already found everything.

Feeling around in unfamiliar cupboards in the dark. Filling egg cups with tap water for my contact lenses. Using a stranger's toothbrush, hating myself, although not enough to risk waking up with rancid breath next to a guy I might want to see a second time. My '80s youth peaked long before these twenty-somethings were born yet it still had a heartbeat. *Ariel, exercise your freedom! Enjoy every minute.* I made a mental note to buy a new toothbrush. *Don't get pregnant.*

I was in my fifties. Divorced. Would they call me single again once the divorce had clocked up more years than the marriage? 'Til the language of patriarchy do us part. Write down my age and people imagine grandchildren, an empty nest, companionable sex with a husband of thirty years. But in the narrative of a good Generation X woman's life, I'd gone so far off script

Share House Story

they didn't have words for me or my relationship. I slept over at my boyfriend's house a few nights a week; I had to reboot my prime-time bedroom moves without the original cast member, oestrogen; and I assessed my commitment to a man by the price-point of cosmetics I was willing to leave at his place.

As far as I could tell, Ariel hadn't even brought a handbag.

One morning, sometime in 1987, my housemate rang me. The era of wall phones, big hair, criminalised abortions. She whispered, 'I have no idea where I am. Maybe Mt Lawley. I won't know until I go outside and see a street sign. I'll take a look once my hangover wears off.' We laughed and laughed. Stories to tell our granddaughters.

Thanks to Google Maps, Ariel wouldn't ever make such a memory. I wondered what kind of story she'd create out of today; if she'd laugh about it with her housemates and tell it so often that it would belong equally to all of them. A fixture in their shared past. Or perhaps, like Josh and Emily, she lived at home and walked the tightrope of work-study-love while trying to keep her parents at a clueless distance. How—if at all—would Ariel include me in this scene? *And making her debut as the cringey father's recently exclusive, try-hard partner...*

The mate snored on the couch. The door to Emily's room was still shut. In the kitchen, I put four teabags into four cups. Boiled water.

Josh emerged and wouldn't look his dad in the eye. 'Don't come into my room.'

'I thought there might be a problem,' his dad said. 'I wanted to help.'

'Then don't do anything,' Josh hissed.

I reached across the decades and handed Ariel a cup of tea.

Half-baked History

Ange Yang

'We have to make Anzac biscuits,' I announce, barrelling through the door of our brown-brick suburban home. I look like a glorified highlighter—my jet-black hair in a bowl cut sitting atop my bright orange uniform, hanging from my chicken-scratch frame.

My popo (grandmother) is at the table, eyes darting between the backpack I'd flung carelessly to the ground and the smudge of dirt on my face, cataloguing the stains that need soaking with a raise of a tattooed eyebrow.

'What's that?'

'A-N-Z-A-C,' I spell out carefully. I pause, scoffing down the bowl of cut apple before me. 'It's got oats in it. They had it in the war—that's why there's no school tomorrow.'

I am too young to comprehend what *war* is. I am oblivious to the cracks in the history that are fed to me from the confines of the school mat and can't comprehend the complications of visas or borders. Conflict is fighting—and fighting is watching Gohan defeat Cell in the latest episode of *Dragon Ball Z* on Cheez TV before going to school. Migration is still something that birds—not people—do.

Popo listens to my recount of the Anzac biscuit eagerly, her hair neatly pinned up in rollers, a damp towel around her neck hanging like a talisman against the Australian sun. Her hands, calloused from rinsing rice and her crusade against dust in our house, extract the crumpled recipes from the depths of my backpack. These are carefully folded, corners cut to fit into an exercise book and tucked next to the microwave.

'*Hao*,' she replies, gingerly plucking the biscuits from the doggy bag. 'Tomorrow. Maybe Sat-*ahh*-day, ok?'

When Saturday arrives with its lazy morning and pop music videos, I balance on the countertop and listen to her jade bangle clack against the bowl of oats and sugar she stirs.

'Clockwise,' I say, twirling my fingers in a circle. 'That's how Mrs Jo did it!'

The small twist of her mouth shows how accustomed she is to my bravado. Still, she dutifully stirs in one direction with the same confidence she has whenever she is in the kitchen.

This is our weekend cooking routine. Popo cracks eggs like a whip and beats them into submission with a practised whisk, her proficiency in the kitchen a fluent language throughout her years of migration from Penang to Perth. Thanks to her skills, our weekend baking routine is never lost in translation, despite the gaps between my Mandarin (which stubbornly stays at the level of a two-year-old) and her rudimentary understanding of English.

With each recipe we stick into the exercise book, each baking tray we line, and each cup of flour we eyeball, I morph into the teacher and she becomes the student. Each school event, carnival or playdate unearths a new discovery.

School morning teas teach her that it is perfectly acceptable to serve raw matchsticks of vegetables—a rude shock coming from a cuisine where vegetables are mostly blanched, steamed or fried. Fairy bread at birthday parties is met with disapproval until I say it's just like mum's favourite snack of buttered toast with raw sugar. Her eyes light up at the peanut butter biscuits I bring home, reminiscent of the peanut crackers in Lunar New Year snack boxes.

It doesn't matter that I can only say a handful of words in Mandarin. We are united by our love of malty Milo drinks, whether hot with condensed milk or piled high atop a glass of cold milk. Vegemite is fondly stirred into congee, mixed into soups, and lauded for its salty soy sauce–like goodness, without the mess of a liquid.

Not all lessons go smoothly. Our failures range from overflowing puddles of molten, would-be lava cakes, to sticky caramel burnt to the sides of a saucepan. There's also the time I come home in tears thinking we were making porridge at school, only to be shocked by the oatmeal soft mess—nothing like the rice porridge she makes.

Ange Yang

The moments and history lessons we share over the rolling boil of a saucepan, and the laughter that bubbles from the bitter taste of wonky biscuits, remain steamed into my memory. Even as she's forgetting them each day.

A Limestone Cottage, with a Skylight to the Stars

Rachelle Erzay

When I was young, my father was a great castle. Made up of impenetrable walls, solid limestone bricks and grand halls. Crafted with tough love, his foundations sunk into the earth with the stubborn intent to stay.

When I'd run through his corridors in a dress of pink tulle, golden chandeliers would light the grand ballrooms. When I'd smear his walls with crayon and chalk, the corridors would chill my bones, and then frame the scribbles later. And when I dared to play on the turrets, his gutters would groan in protest. Sometimes he'd catch me if I slipped, and sometimes he'd let me fall; lessons learnt the hard way.

As I grew older, the castle grew smaller, corridors tighter and stones cooler. His halls were quiet, doors locked more often. I'd spend my days in the courtyard, gazing up at the box of sky, wondering whether it would unfold itself down to a place I could reach. Those days, he was both sanctuary and confinement, safety and smothering. My voice would echo—notes bouncing to nowhere and everywhere. I'd call in the clouds and wild storms would rage within, but the water would run straight off his stones.

When I cut my hair, we both knew the time had come. His gates opened wide and I forgot to look back. The air was a sprig of fresh mint, and the sun a bright, burning flame. For once, I could follow the sky and keep going. Years passed, and I fell in and out of love with those who carried a castle's chill. The more I searched for walls, bricks and grounding in others, the more I longed to return to a past that didn't exist anymore. It was only when I started to lay my own foundations that I felt ready to return.

Now, he is starting to crumble. The stones of his structure are weathered and pockmarked. The years have been kind, but they are still years lost. I may no longer dance in his great halls or play on his turrets, but I visit for tea from time to time, patching where I can, refurbishing what he'll let me. And someday soon when he falls into ruin, I know he'll be proud of the home I've become.

Wouldn't You Rather Be in the Kitchen?

Danielle Berryman

In the 1970s my dad—bemused by my interest and under sufferance—taught me a few manly skills. My younger brother and I learnt to use hand drills, the vice and C-clamps, how to plane wood and chip out wedges with a chisel. To 'measure twice and cut once.'

The highlight of time in the shed was learning to use the arc welder—a volatile machine with unlimited opportunities for failure. We could have caused a fire! We risked slag burns to our clothes and skin; flash burns if the giant helmet slipped from our small heads or we forgot to close the visor.

Worse still, I could disappoint Dad by over-welding a hole or clumping welds into an untidy mess. I treasured my time in the shed but knew it was an uneasy thing that could be taken away at any moment. There were reminders in Dad's question: 'Wouldn't you rather be with your mother in the kitchen?'

'Hell no!' I would have said if swearing had been allowed. Bombe alaska couldn't compare to a sparking welding rod in an arena of high expectations. All food did was disappear into people's mouths and had to be made again a couple of hours later. In the shed we built useful things that would last.

My heroes were mostly men, apart from Katherine Hepburn who was feisty and wore trousers, and Audrey Hepburn who fit with my love of heels, makeup and fashion, especially the vintage op-shop finds I mixed and matched with hand-me-downs. Both actresses were witty and sophisticated, with compassion and endearing fallibility.

After a weekend TV screening of *Hatari* I longed to run away to Africa and work with wild animals—and John Wayne! Half of me wanted to be the actor, while the other half wanted to fall in love with him. Not the conservative 'Duke' persona but his Sean Mercer character from *Hatari*, a pushover prone to falling eye-rollingly in love with an emotional, creative fish out of water.

Beyond the shed there were plenty of life skills to be learnt: building a fire, changing tyres, tying on fish hooks and sinkers, setting a line and driving boats and cars.

Once we drove an old Holden station wagon to Three Springs so it could become a farm car for our cousins. The Holden travelled well. After we'd arrived, my brother and I had some driving practice along the kilometre between the front gate and the house. A minute after I took over, someone spotted a wheel rolling into the paddock before the car listed to the left, bare axle ploughing into the dirt. The wheel nuts had been loosening all the way from Perth and had finally jumped free. I'd been driving slowly and had been taught not to panic. Still, the incident quickly became a funny family story in which I took some ribbing about driving like a girl and wrecking the car.

At sixteen, my first 'proper' driving lesson was in Kardinya's shopping centre carpark on a Saturday afternoon. These were the days when the shops closed at midday and the bitumen was deserted. We were in Dad's work ute and he was nervous about it getting damaged.

'If in doubt, all out!' he instructed me after explaining the pedal arrangement three times. In other words, hit the brakes and clutch if danger arises. I was doing well but Dad's nerves got the better of him and he started to panic about a tree between two empty bays a hundred metres away. 'Look out for that tree! Don't get too close!'

'Dad, that's miles away.' I steered to the left at the terrifying speed of twelve km an hour in first gear.

'Look out! Look out!' he shouted as we edged to within eighty metres of the tree. 'All out! All out!' he cried at the fifty-metre mark, and I gave up, easing on the brake and clutch and coming to a full stop, at which point Dad yanked on the handbrake.

We swapped seats and he took time to catch his breath, wiping his face with his hanky, before driving us home. 'I'll let your mother teach you from now on,' he said on arrival. We never spoke of it again.

London Brawling

Greig Johnston

None of it was normal. A forty-one-year-old man in the company of an eight-year-old boy. An all-night coach from Glasgow to London. A fight for the heavyweight championship of the world, held at 1 am to suit American TV.

Many of the finer points escape me now, but what I can tell you is that the eight-year-old me did not have an iPad. As a parenting move, it could be described as outlandish. My father, now nudging eighty, was making an incredible leap of faith with regard to my attention span. The thought of undertaking a similar trip with my own kids, without digital anaesthetic, makes me sweat.

The trip has been largely erased. All I remember is the strip lighting in the McDonald's, where my dad got me a cheeseburger nearing midnight. We spilled out of the bus into a London dawn, and the first people I saw were two heavily leathered punks—this was 1986—with huge, spiked hair, sprawled on a bench.

'Have you got any fucking smokes?' one said to the other. My father's grip on my hand became progressively tighter until we found a taxi.

London Brawling

The purpose of the trip was one Mr Franklin Roy Bruno, an English heavyweight contender who rivalled the Pope in popularity. Bruno ('Big Frank' as he was known in our house) was massive—a magnetic personality and a concussive puncher. His post-fight interviews with commentator Harry Carpenter—punctuated by his catchphrase 'Know what I mean 'Arry?'—were top shelf entertainment and had turned him into a British folk hero. In the fight before his shot at the heavyweight title, a few of his right hands had sent former champion Gerrie Coetzee into a brisk sleep, sprawled over the ringside press photographers. Now, Bruno would face the American Tim Witherspoon for the title. In our minds Big Frank could not be denied.

The first shadows of doubt appeared in the cab, when the jocular East Ender driving began talking to my dad.

'You down for the fight?' he asked.

'Yep, me and the boy've got tickets,' my dad said.

'You fink Frank can do it?'

'Yep, no doubt about it,' my dad said.

'Ooooooh I wish I had your confidence mate. I worry he's a bit chinny.'

My dad said nothing, just looked out the window of the cab.

We went on a small-scale tour of London. I was underwhelmed by Buckingham Palace and overwhelmed by Hamleys, the biggest toy shop in the world.

At some point, although I could not tell you how, we made our way to Wembley Stadium, where 40,000 mostly British and mostly drunk people had gathered to roar the hometown hero on.

'B r u u u u u u u u u u u u u u u u u u u u u u n o o o. Bruuuuuuuuuuuuuuuuuuunooo,' they called with the volume of an airliner taking off.

I remember climbing a lot of stairs and when we arrived at our seats, we were in danger of altitude sickness. I turned around and tried to find the ring.

I needed a power nap, but sometime around 1 am the sound of those 40,000 drunks roused me. My dad leaned down and, with wonder in his eyes, told me Muhammad Ali was somewhere down there.

When the fight got underway, all I could make out were two dots moving slowly around the ring. The crowd, those that could actually see, seethed and pulsed with the action.

Then late in the eleventh round, though I couldn't have told you that then, one of the dots—the dot that was Bruno—stopped moving and for a moment every kilojoule of energy was sucked out of that stadium. My father's hand wrapped around mine and pulled me out of my seat as the atmosphere became slightly hostile.

We swam across town, back to our hotel, for a few hours blessed sleep before the bus left.

The next morning, we got an early march on the buffet. We sat down for our bacon and eggs, saying little. There was a sudden bombast, in that way only an American accent can pollute your surroundings. He was an older gentleman, at the table opposite us.

London Brawling

'Did you watch the fight last night?' he said, sounding like JR out of *Dallas*.

'Yeah,' my dad said.

'You know ... I think the guy just ran outta gas.'

My old man smiled at me. Other fathers and sons would have fishing or camping trips, driving lessons or chess. But me and my old man would always have Wembley, and Big Frank Bruno just running out of gas.

A Medley of Love Songs

Gillian O'Shaughnessy

Does Your Mother Know?

You blag your way past the bouncers with your fake ID and a smile, slug down a beer, feeling taller with each swallow. A guy from the band gleams your way from over near the bar so you blow him a kiss. You're fresh, you're Lolita, you're a Cherry Coke charm. He picks his way across the room, maybe he'll buy you a drink or ask for your number, but he pushes in close, pants in your face like a dog. His spit sprays, his breath is sour and before you can move, he shoves his hand between your legs, squeezes hard through your jeans. He floats off, casual as a cloud on a blue-sky summer day.

What's New, Pussycat?

You finish your shift at the pancake parlour late, walk through the park to the bus stop. Firmly gripping your handbag, you keep to pools of lamplight; it spills in yellow circles on the grass. You sense a presence behind you, feel a trickle of fear, maybe it's nothing, maybe you should turn your head, take off your heels and run. Instead, you keep a steady pace, try to look strong. Unafraid. You feel a rush of air, a sharp shove to your back, you stagger. A man you don't know waves his hand in your face. Laughs aloud at the joke. He says, *scared you, didn't I?*

Are You Lonesome Tonight?

He doesn't take it well when you leave him. He phones over and over into the night, shows up at work, leaves notes in the letterbox, he wants you to know he is watching, he wants you to know he can hurt you. You call the police; they turn up but there's *not a lot they can do is there? He hasn't done anything illegal.* Then one says *look—we can drop by tomorrow, make sure everything's ok, give you some advice on a VRO* and you say *thanks, Officer.* He comes back alone, asks how things are, says *maybe we should go out sometime* and you go *sure, maybe sometime.* When he pulls up again, blue lights flashing, you hide behind the door. Wait for the sound of his boots to retreat up the path.

What's Love Got to Do with It?

You don't want to go out with him, he won't take no for an answer. He follows you in his beat-up yellow stick-shift Holden, he says *c'mon baby get in, you know you want to, get in, save us messing around. Get in. Get in.* You walk a little faster and he pulls onto the curb and across the pavement, cutting off your exit. He opens the door, tilts his head down in a way he clearly thinks is appealing. He asks again, you say no again. He unzips his jeans, holds his flaccid cock in his fist and says *how about now.*

Am I Ever Gonna See Your Face Again?

It's 2 am and he's not home. Third time this week and you've got work in the morning. He calls, eventually. Drunk-sad, slurring his words, he's at that spot on the river, looking down at the water, says everything would be better if he wasn't around. You want to sleep but you pull on your coat, find your car keys, head out to the bridge. There's no one there. An empty tram rattles past on its last trip from the city and you wonder what you're doing out here. Tomorrow, you'll find a small black bra hidden in his work bag, and you'll know it doesn't belong to you. You'll put it back where you found it. Get an early night.

Forever Eleven

Brodi Snook

I stand in front of the 'Sanitary Care' wall at the pharmacy, overwhelmed.

IS *YOUR* PERIOD GREEN? shouts a box of twelve-dollar bamboo pads, accusingly. When I started menstruating as a teenager, my mother told me to use code words on the shopping list, so I wouldn't disgust my father and brother. Pads were 'surfboards' until I left home at eighteen.

Swayed by the 'reduced' price sticker, I flick a home brand packet of tampons into my basket, knowing they'll feel like suppositories made of sandpaper. I can feel eyes upon me, so pervasive they might as well be hands. A few metres away, a goateed stranger scans the length of me, as though he is quality checking a product. I stare at the shelf, pins and needles tickling my palms. I can almost see the thought bubble above his thickly gelled head: *WOULD I?* I feel threatened, yet also desperate to pass the test.

I was eleven years old when I first got cat-called. It was the winter school holidays; I had been op-shopping with my friend Meg. Perusing the moth-balled tatters at charity shops was a sacred weekend pastime for country kids, along with catching tadpoles and attempting seances while our parents were down the pub, trying to relinquish their own ghosts. Meg and I would pool our chore shrapnel and disappear into the maze of clothing racks at Vinnies, trying on every shoulder-padded, stale-smelling item someone's nan had recently carked it in. Donning itchy woollen knits, we would twist and turn in the changing-room mirror, planning the women we would be by the time they fit us. Meg was going to move to Paris and be a nanny. I was going to be an Olympic soccer player, just like Alison Forman.

After a morning spent clattering around the shop aisles in stilettos, we sat on the kerb and pored over our bounty from the bargain bin. Meg inspected her chipped floral tea set that her mum would obligingly make room for in their kitchen cabinet. I marvelled over my Ripper '77 record, the profane cover of which would stay tacked to my bedroom door well into my twenties.

A small four-wheel drive filthy with orange dirt clumsily rounded the corner. Four boys spilled from its windows, making indecipherable noise. The P-plater slowed down as his front-seat passenger pointed toward us, cross-legged on the pavement and lovingly handling our new treasures.

'I wouldn't fuck ya, ya mingers!'

Hoarse honking echoed down the street as the car sped off, taking our innocence with it. The adulthood we were so enchanted by had been foisted upon us, too soon. With one careless slur, we had gone from little girls playing grown-ups to young women convinced there was something wrong with us. We giggled reflexively, already in training for a lifetime of self-abandonment. I don't recall another op-shopping day after that. Maybe we never went again. Maybe we quickly swapped our babyish dress-ups for more sophisticated excursions, like hanging out at the skatepark, waiting to be noticed.

I saw Meg last year at a schoolmate's engagement party and wanted to quiz her about her memory of this violation. My penchant for picking at the scabs of childhood wounds is the reason I am seldom invited to these events. I didn't get the opportunity; she left early to take her too-pissed husband home. I hope she's been to Paris. I gave up playing soccer in high school after being informed by the boys that it was exclusively for lesbians.

The leering man kisses his teeth and dawdles over to 'Dental Care'. I return my reduced tampons to the shelf and follow him, suddenly needing floss.

Are Three Underpants Enough?

Pia Russo

'Huh?' I reply with knitted eyebrows. I ponder, *where is Mum's head now*? I'm trying to concentrate on driving.

'Should I buy more underpants or are three enough?'

'Enough for what?'

'You know.'

'No.'

'Well, I might not last much longer. Will they tide me over till I'm gone?'

'Oh, Mum. Not that again.'

She has proclaimed her imminent end ever since Dad died—for nine birthdays, nine Mother's Days, and nine Christmases. She's still here. But I won't labour the point.

'You should treat yourself and buy three more.'

And that's where we drive to next.

The Day He Died

Mabel Gibson

When my mum answered the phone she fell down on her knees. She looked just like a small child. I'd never seen her not be brave but I was only eleven. I remember it as a winter's day, even though it was November. It rained inside my house, my mother's eyes replaced the sky. And when she finally said that he was dead I felt like she had drowned me. I spent the night at the family computer googling heroin. And I wished that I could take his place because my mum already has three daughters and she needed her brother. I felt the inside of my brain change from innocent to grown. The world had stopped, the colours dulled and I was expected to keep going. And there he was everywhere, haunting me in my teenage bedroom. Grief is a bad tattoo you get when things are kind of blurry—a permanent reminder of my mother screaming. And now I'm almost twenty-four and I've lived several lives, but I've found grief has stuck around as my most loyal friend. Because I can't forget the day he died and the way my mother looked. I'll spend my life as an eleven-year-old child drowning in my mother's tears.

Summer, 1981

Louise Burlinson

Summer's soundtrack is on repeat: the wash of waves on the shore, the bent-neck, indignant arguing of seagulls over sandy chips, and the laughter of cousins. We've all got sandy feet, and salt-kissed hair tickles our browning shoulders.

'What day is it?'

Clutching precious coins turning sweaty in my palm, we trek up the beach to the kiosk on Andersons Wharf. We round the corner and stomp up the wooden stairs. Do we have enough silver for a Paddle Pop? Chocolate or rainbow? *Not* banana. Or maybe an icy pole? These are weighty decisions.

'But I don't want to go home.'

On endless cousin-filled play days, we kneel and build sandcastles with dribbled sand turrets. Castle moats are scraped out by small, familiar hands. The water's coming! Let's dig right through to the other side of the world. Time for another swim.

Diesel, fishing gear and the salt-crusted nets of the boatshed. Watch the gutting knife. Old fish scales, tiny flat jewels, pepper the grass. Permanent sunshine as the days stretch on forever like the blue skies. Tomorrow,

Summer, 1981

if we're lucky, we might find a seahorse bobbing in the weed.

'Not yet, Mum.'

There is lemonade. Turned into Fire Engines by the alchemy of cochineal colouring in Duralex glasses. Guess the tiny number hidden at the bottom. Fish (that we caught) and chips for dinner. Nana's face breaks into a beaming, shell-pink smile. Elnett and powdery perfumed hugs.

'No. Please don't take me home!'

The Unfortunate Die Twice

Ying Xiong (David) Goh

'Swimming, swimming, is it going to be swimming today?'

She looks out the window and points at the sky. It's getting more and more difficult to understand her speech but often, with context, it's still manageable. She repeats herself, becoming more agitated by the moment.

'Swimming, swimming, is it swimming today?'

I hear the tumbling of the laundry as the washing machine enters into its final spin cycle. Ours is an old one and every washing cycle makes it seem like it's about to go into a mechanical seizure.

It always takes a while, but the context arrives. An uninspiring epiphany.

'Do you mean if it's going to rain today?'

'Yes, yes, is it swimming today?'

'No, Ma, it's not. You can put the clothes out in the open today.'

I can see the frustration when she tries to express herself, but that ability has been taken away from her. She is akin to a child, having needs and wants, but lacking the vocabulary to say what she means.

The Unfortunate Die Twice

The most obvious physical change is perhaps in her eyes. She's had dark brown eyes for as long as I can remember but with the onset of the condition, the dark brown of her irises have been tinged with an ominous grey. It envelopes the outer circumference and, as each year passes, eats greedily into the inner layers. When I look into her eyes, I see an emptiness forming. If the eyes are the seat of the soul, would this imply that her soul is slowly being chipped away? Is the soul just a composition of our memories formed over time? When all of it has withered away and only the body remains, will she still be my mother? When I cremate the body of my mother, will it just be a shell that I am cremating? Is my mother both her soul and her body? What is it that I mourn? The death of her soul or the death of her body?

She is not the same person as she was before the condition.

When she married my father, she knew he suffered from severe depression. Despite being given counsel by my grandmother to not marry him, she still chose him. Over the decades of their marriage, he made multiple attempts on his own life, and at every failed attempt, it was my mother that remained by his side. At no point did she question her duty to him as a wife and her responsibility as a mother to their children.

When there were internal conflicts with the extended family, she was always the sibling that bore the brunt of the emotional toll. At no point did she question her duty as a sister to her siblings and her responsibility as a daughter to her parents.

As her behaviour shifts and is now characterised by words like uncaring, selfish, sharp, hurtful, demeaning, I begin to wonder—was she always like this as a person? Has she always had these thoughts? Has the condition broken away her inhibitions to reveal her true nature? Or has the condition robbed her of her strength to battle the corrupt and corrosive nature that is inherent in every person? Is goodness not the absence of evil but the triumph over it? I want to believe that my mother was a good person. I want to believe that my mother *is* a good person.

'I'm so tired. My body hurts everywhere. It is very easy to leave the world.'

These are the cruel moments of clarity which are afforded her. As her fatigue grows ever stronger, she has a tendency to take naps often, usually on a couch in the living room. Sometimes, I stand there, watching her. She breathes in, she breathes out. Perhaps there could be a merciful end to this cruel fate. She breathes in, she breathes out.

My Letterbox

Lauren McLennan

When I was eight years old, I had my own letterbox. It was made from an empty plain blue tissue carton and a cardboard roll holder discarded from its previous job of dispensing paper towels. It lived outside my bedroom door and each day after school I would stuff my hand into the box to see what mail had been delivered.

I was a hairy child. Most European children are adorned with facial hair, but my eyebrows were the talk of my classmates. It wasn't the monobrow that bothered people; it was the fact that hair also grew in the space between my eyebrow arch and my eyelids. I didn't know that twenty years later hairy brows could have made me a D-list celebrity who spruiked beauty products from paid sponsorships. At the time I was sad about being bullied.

I don't remember telling my family, but they figured out what was going on and I came home one day to see my letterbox overflowing with mail. A letter from my mum told me not to worry about mean people from school. My brother just drew a picture of my face with an arrow pointing to eyebrows, but it was funny when he teased me. My sister wrote something about me being better than all those stupid people in my year. Dad wrote that everyone in my class was a 'billy' (as in silly). He wrote in all capital letters and signed off like this: DAD. I kept every letter in a special box in the bottom of my chest of drawers.

I must have stopped receiving mail one afternoon. I couldn't tell you the exact moment we all grew out of it. It did take me twenty years to grow into my eyebrows and to stop over-plucking them.

139 Yale Rd

Kyeesha Bonney

The run-down brown house at the end of the street was ours.

The inside was just as run down as the outside, unpleasant in every aspect. Walls that looked more yellow than white made everything seem more crowded than it was. Our house was uncomfortably open, missing curtains and furniture mainly because they were used as weapons in their arguments or a boxing bag in her fits of rage.

The door that joined our half to theirs, come nightfall, was a turquoise green—meaning it had been replaced. Still, there was a man-sized hole through the middle of it, horribly taped up to try and retain privacy. Yet their voices echoed through our half, filling up our silent nights.

The stale smell of alcohol lingered through the entire house, in constant war with the bitter tasting scent of gunja.

I remember the surround-sound that came in handy for their parties, playing songs I grew up to love, before it too became a victim of their arguments and her rage once again.

The Window

Philippa Freegard

'When I was your age, it was 1918,' she says. 'Do you know about the Great War?'

I am turning twelve when she asks me this, as she deftly knits a sweater for one of my many cousins. She is seventy-two. Her hands are gnarled and shiny, and although she still has many more years to live, to me she is unfathomably old. I struggle and fail to picture my bent-over, diminutive grandmother as she must have been six decades earlier. Had she looked like me? In sixty years' time, will I be then as she is now?

'I used to be sent to help Auntie Dolly,' she continues. 'Auntie Dolly had raised six sons. Six sons, and not a single daughter! She was on her own in the cottage.'

'There was a lot of laundry. She had to take in other people's you see, just to survive. She would boil it all up in the copper, dry it in the little yard at the back, and then iron it beautifully.' The folding was a good reason for Nan to escape the crowded two-up, two-down that held her mother, her drunken veteran father and her five siblings. It was warm and dry in Dolly's front room, and when the work was done there was a promised cup of cocoa in the snug kitchen behind.

The Window

'Auntie Dolly would have been in her late forties,' Nan says, pulling more wool onto her lap as she gives a little sigh. 'By that point in the Great War, her husband and five—*five*—of her six sons had died in the trenches of France.'

I try to imagine the husband and sons, lying motionless in the French mud. And my twelve-year-old Nan, folding snow-white sheets and pillowcases.

'You know,' Nan says, 'I always remember this one time I went to help Auntie Dolly. We were in the front room as usual, and she was ironing away. In those days, you didn't have an electric iron. You had two heavy old black irons and you had to stand them in front of the fire to heat up, until they were hot enough to use. You would swap one for the other when the first one cooled off.'

Her eyes, already a little cloudy from nascent cataracts, glisten slightly. Then she snaps her gaze back onto me, her fingers not ceasing their knitting and purling. 'You might have seen one of those irons in a museum,' she says, nodding slightly. 'As I say, on that morning I was helping Auntie Dolly, and she was ironing by the window—beautiful linen sheets and tablecloths, from the doctor's house. Dolly was talking and ironing, talking and ironing. I was folding table napkins by the fire. And then suddenly, she just stopped, right in the middle of saying something. I looked up at her, and she was staring out the window, with the hot iron still in her hand. I followed her gaze and saw someone coming up the garden path—a young lad with a bag on his shoulder. Well, I recognised him straight away. It was Sam Heasman, the young telegram boy. Not much older than me. And then—here's something odd, my duck—I remember there was this funny sort of pause, which went on for ages. As if everything was just suspended; Sam on the path, Auntie Dolly stopped in her work, and me looking at her.

'And then, Auntie Dolly drew the iron back as far as her arm would let her, and she hurled it with all her might straight through the window.

'There was a terrible noise. It was the smashing of glass and a howl all mixed up together. She knew you see, my duck. Somehow, she already knew what was in that telegram. The news that her sixth and only surviving son had been killed. Billy, he was called. He was seventeen. I remember that noise like it was yesterday.'

She puts her knitting to one side now. She fixes me in her gaze, and I understand, wordlessly, that she is handing something over. That this story of stasis and chaos will remain with me, that the nuances I cannot fully intuit at twelve will nonetheless endure and resonate as I get older, that the resonance will become louder still when I have a son of my own. That Dolly's story will be retold.

Austerity

Alice Macri

Her voice was husky and sweet, like treacle tart, as she told me stories about growing up during World War II.

She spoke of helping her mother tape newspapers over the windows so that if the bombs dropped and the glass exploded, it wouldn't shatter inwards. A patchwork of news articles filtered out the sunlight, reflecting headlines of conflict across the linoleum floor.

She reminisced about standing on a stool as her mother measured her for clothes made from the amber-coloured curtains. The material was scratchy and the pattern was gaudy, but her growing body wouldn't wait for peace time.

She told me of her mum teaching her how to embroider, so that they could repurpose old bed sheets as tablecloths. About how she begged her mother to bake a cake with the remaining eggs they traded a cabbage for, rather than keeping them for breakfast. She spoke of darning her socks and air raid drills and ration tickets.

Her father was away, as all the capable young men were. She was a daddy's girl, and her brothers griped about how she was the favourite. She missed him dearly and prayed for his return.

Alice Macri

The battle began when the man who returned wasn't the father who left. He had become cold and irascible, speaking to the children as if they were soldiers. They grappled with the two different versions of the man they admired.

She recalled a night when her brother, John, spoke back to him at the dinner table. The argument itself was long forgotten, but burnt into her mind was how the candle flame extinguished with the sheer force of her father's bellowing. John—'bull-headed idiot that he was'—wouldn't surrender. Her mother urged them both to calm down, her serviette hanging from her right hand like a white flag.

'Dad leapt across the table and decked John across the mouth. Crack!' she said, with a clap. I jumped, dropping the weed puller. 'His lip started gushing red all over the tablecloth and my mum screamed bloody murder. My dad just got up from the table, walked out the back with his smokes, and slammed the door.'

She wiped the sweat from her brow as we took a break from digging the doublegees out of her grass. It was the first warm day we'd had in months. I had forgotten to use sunscreen and could already feel the first sting of a sunburn across my back.

'Looking back now, I can tell that we weren't the family he wanted anymore. He had met someone while deployed, and when the end of the war came, he didn't want to come back. That's why he was so explosive all

Austerity

the time. But we didn't know … How could we have known?'

She took a long drink from a can of Diet Coke. The perspiration dripped down her long, knobbly fingers.

'No matter how hard she tried, my mum never could get the blood out of that tablecloth.'

Sunday Gherkins

Andrew Tetlaw

'Mum, can I have a gherkin?'

It was Sunday afternoon and my brother took the initiative and was at Mum's bedroom door, raising his voice to be heard.

We knew the closed door was a warning to us not to disturb.

An important mission: we were hungry, and the jars of Mum's homemade gherkins were lined up on a pantry shelf. Sweet, green, and crunchy.

There was no reply. Undeterred, he changed tactics, manoeuvring himself onto the verandah that ran around the perimeter of the house. An open bedroom window offered an angle of approach and he climbed up to the window sill.

'Mum, can I have a gherkin?'

It was the gruff, bearded voice of our stepfather I heard next:

'Fuck off!'

I don't remember eating gherkins that day.

The Last Pieces

Shannon Brie

I have a secret stash of photographs in our garage. They lie like crouching tigers in tall grass, ready to pounce.

There's about a dozen of them inside a crinkled white DL peel-and-seal envelope. This paper barrier keeps their stench from infecting the surrounding piles of innocent, acceptable photographs.

The envelope that houses them is unsealed; the flimsy plastic tab still affixed, ready to be exposed in a moment of me forgetting what's in there. On those occasions I am rummaging through storage boxes, looking for a different memory. In my hands they break the surface, an orca searching for air, and my stomach turns, my chest tightens. I look at them with sombre compulsion then tuck them back inside.

Our garage is a suburban cave, and our possessions are drop bears in hibernation. Remnants of the past are stacked on each industrial shelf in clear, plastic tubs with bright blue snap-lock handles. The things we don't use are banished here. The things we can't throw away. Faded Fraggle with half an eye. A collection of CDs that belonged to my mother. Tennis rackets that need restringing. My son's first pair of sandal shoes.

I like labels. They provide an anchor on those days when the world spins beneath my feet, threatening to toss me akilter. It's meditative, like organisational yoga. I take a label, write a title, breathe … remove the sticky part, align it symmetrically on the receiving object, attach it firmly, breathe. If a stranger was to walk through our garage, they would know immediately where to find the dog toys, Christmas decorations and Sweet Valley books. And the three tubs of photos.

Inside these tubs are sub-levels of attempted orderliness. Unfinished albums, undeveloped rolls of film, and piles of loose photographs held together by yellowing rubber bands and willpower. A piece of paper tucked inside the band decrees the theme of each pile.

Pets. Holidays. Family.

Except for that pile, that envelope. It has no title. Like the Hogwarts wizarding community in fear of its villain, I dare not speak its name.

'Your garage is so neat!' my friend exclaimed.

'All the better to park our cars,' I replied.

I didn't say, 'Stay right there, don't look too closely at my secrets,' but I thought it—my heart racing.

I think we would have burnt them if it weren't for the potentially noxious fumes that would release. Or perhaps it just wasn't worth the mental effort. All I knew was that she needed them gone. I knew this innately,

The Last Pieces

without her saying so or asking me. So I went through her photographs, one by one, and plucked out everything that showed his face.

I did not betray her that day. I sat on the rug of her Ascot home, diligently discarding photos, erasing my father from our lives. In that moment, I too wished him gone. My mum had discovered that she gave thirty-eight years of love to a thief, and I had learnt why it always felt like he was somewhere else. Because he had been. For over three decades, he had been in the arms of other women. Married women whose children I had played with, who had sat at our family dining table, laughing with my mother and helping her clear the dishes.

At her funeral, he was not mentioned in the eulogy, nor did he feature in the photographic tribute. We made sure of that. His prominent chapter in her life was a cruelty, and for those who love her, he is anathema. I cannot forgive the pain he inflicted, the remorse he does not feel, the time he stole.

My sister and I spent an afternoon selecting photos that would best celebrate our mum's life. That's when I found them. Turned out I had missed a few, all those years ago. I silently slipped them aside and took them home with me.

The last pieces of our whole family. A heavily pregnant mother standing beside a seemingly adoring husband with 1970s-style sideburns. A father looking exhausted, cradling a red-faced, bloated newborn me in his arms. My mother on her wedding day, her long dark hair cascading down her shoulders. All of us smiling at my twenty-first birthday brunch.

Crouching in that envelope is my estranged father, who I love.

Notes of J.C.L.

Ana Lynch

It's empty.

Nearly. This house, their house, our used-to-be home. My brothers and I return, the space reeking of bleach and disinfectant instead of the scent of lamb roast. Just the cupboards to go. We pack big lives into small cardboard boxes and stolen milk crates. I chuck years of *I'll use that one day* into the skip bin in the driveway. We stuff heavy woollen blankets from our childhood into big green garbage bags, along with a broken rolling pin, stacks of dog-eared *Reader's Digest*, other worn ordinary things. We swap stories, and memories come like morse dots and dashes with years in between.

We move from room to room, until there is only one left. I open the bedroom wardrobe and see his clothes. I go slowly now, one coat hanger at a time. I slip my hand into the inside pocket of his favourite club jacket—smooth cool satin, its maroon glory faded. A handkerchief. *A gentleman always carries one.* I touch the crisply ironed lines of the forest green linen, black embroidery in a flourish: J.C.L. I hold it to my cheek, my nose, and inhale a cloud of my father, John. A base note of Wee Willem cigar, a heart note of Old Spice aftershave, a salted top note of Sunday beach mornings.

I take a time-tumble. I'm six years old, Dad sitting on my white embroidered chenille bedspread, telling stories of Bib and Bub roaming eucalypt forests and granite rock holes in search of lost children. Venturing barefoot through gloomy, slime-water swamps. Baking bread in the bush on a weave of green sapling over open coals. It is intoxicating Smell-a-Vision.

At story's end, he kisses my forehead and tucks his hanky into my pyjama cuff. I drift off on a curl of aroma … safe and sound and smoke and spice.

The Water Cycle

Seth Malacari

Step 1: Condensation

A limited selection of things they said to me:
'When we first met, I didn't find you attractive.'
(wet emojis on their ex's selfies)
'Nobody could ever love you the way I do.'
(a message from their ex appears on screen)
'If you start crying, I'll leave.'
(they book a hotel room with their ex-girlfriend)

Step 2: Sublimation

'I love you,' they say in a rehearsed voice. 'You're my soulmate. I only want to be with you, but I need to have sex with other people. I don't want you to have sex with other people though. Is that ok?'

I say it is ok. I spend nights alone crying (I'm sorry). I research polyamory, trying to understand. What is ethical non-monogamy without any ethics?

I am in a one-sided open relationship that I technically consented to. I really wish I hadn't. I stay anyway.

Step 3: Precipitation

It is the day I get braces. They have rated me a 7/10. They said I would look better if my teeth were straight. They are in the kitchen, chopping vegetables. I approach, smiling. I want them to say I am beautiful.

They point the knife at me. 'Get out of my face. I'm so sick of your shit.'

For once, I listen. I walk out the front door.

'If you leave, you can't come back.'

I leave.

Something hits the pavement next to my car. It is a framed photo of my daughter, the glass smashed on the driveway. Next is an armful of my clothes.

'I'm going,' I say. 'Just leave my stuff.'

I get out of the car and plead with them to leave my things alone. I stand on the wet grass between them and our front door. They are right-handed, but they punch with their left. That was the first time.

I come back the next morning. We both say sorry.

Step 4: Transpiration

We sit in my therapist's office. A thriving plant in the corner. The room temperature is perfectly regulated. My therapist, dressed in flowing linen, sits across from us. We sit as far apart as possible while still being on the same couch. They were adamant that they come to my

The Water Cycle

next session to correct all the lies I have been telling about them. They speak in a calm voice. I cry the whole time. My therapist pushes the tissue box across the table to me.

Later, on that same couch, when it's just her and me, my therapist helps me understand I am being abused.

A list of things I realise (unordered)
I was right (psychological).
I definitely said no (sexual).
This is not love (emotional).
I am not a piece of shit (verbal).
It's not my fault (physical).

Step 5: Runoff

I pack my things into my car in a frantic rush.
I pack strange things I don't even need or want.
I hear a car pull up. The sound sends my anxiety spiking.
I race out the front. It is my neighbour. They stare at me with my arms full of useless cables, face puffy and red and tear stained. They go inside without a word.
I drive away from my home. Exhale.
Then the terror spreads through me again.
I turn the car around, recklessly.
I have left my camera behind. The one thing I own that is worth anything. I race inside to get it.
I haven't used that camera since.

Step 6: Evaporation

Day 1.

I sit on the balcony of my safe house and for the first time in two years I actually feel safe. My phone is switched off because blocking them didn't stop them. I light a cigarette. They never liked me to smoke, but it's a guilty pleasure. It is summer. The sky is clear and blue. The sea breeze is in, sending sand and salt across the pavement. Heat radiates off the street below. I smell the pizza restaurant next door firing up the ovens. I write love notes to my future self as the sun beams down upon my skin. I feel the weight evaporate.

Where It Began

Caroline Hayward

I leaned over to kiss her for the very first time. I had not been able to get near her before now. Mum's back was turned, buttering toast. The new baby was lying there, unguarded in her bassinet lined with a white frilled sheet. Nothing of mine was white. The angle of the sun through the window hit the canopy and created an angel's halo.

A few weeks earlier, Dad had swung open the front door proudly, 'We're home!' We leapt up. We'd had enough of Weetbix and wrinkled clothes. We got a quick glance from Mum before the new baby was hurried away out of our reach. The new baby needed to sleep.

Now, the new baby was quietly regarding me. Her unblinking stillness was creepy. I closed my eyes as I moved my face towards her, whispering kindly, 'Hello, baby.'

Bam!

I reeled back. What had hit me? It had come suddenly, without warning. My jaw was slammed shut so violently that I bit my tongue. There might be blood.

I pointed and said through tears, 'She kicked me!' From past experience, the shock in my voice should have roused an immediate response from my mother. It was a few minutes before she came to investigate after first brushing off her hands on a tea towel.

'What happened?' she demanded without looking my way.

Maybe I hadn't been loud enough. 'She kicked me!' I declared with rising indignation.

'I heard you the first time,' Mum said. Her hand came towards me. I thought she wanted to check my injury, so I raised my chin up to her. But she was just moving me aside so she could more easily get to the bassinet. To the new baby. Mum made a cooing sound which was not the remonstration I expected.

Never before had so blatant a crime gone unpunished in our household.

'She kicked me,' I said again.

Mum tsked. 'Don't be ridiculous. She's only a baby. She didn't mean to kick you. It was just a reflex.'

It felt like she didn't want me to get close, that she didn't want to get to know me.

'I only wanted to give her a kiss!' I wailed. I thought Mum would have praised me for my friendly overture and shared my dismay over the fickleness of the baby's affections.

Instead, Mum busied herself with the blanket crocheted by Nana, adjusting it over the new baby's feet while she gurgled cheerfully.

I held on to the thought that Mum would be on my side, would understand my point of view. 'It hurt!'

Where It Began

'Nonsense!' Mum admonished with undue severity. 'She's only a little baby! She isn't strong enough to hurt you!'

How wrong my mother was. The baby was strong enough.

'Just leave the baby alone!' My mother picked up the bassinet and, murmuring soft words, left me to process the rejection all alone.

I did leave the baby alone after that. For a really long time.

The Prosperous Red Phoenix Restaurant

Shirley Marr

The restaurant wasn't much more than a hole in the wall, jammed between a 24-hour chemist and a hairdressing salon. It sat along an arterial highway in a quiet southern Perth suburb that wasn't good, but wasn't the worst by far, as locals would claim. The brick facade was painted red, with an arched doorway and one window in the shape of an octagon. Even as an eight-year-old in the eighties, The Prosperous Red Phoenix looked out of place, like it shouldn't have followed us when we migrated here.

On the inside it was much bigger than expected, with room to fit eight banquet tables, suitable for a modest Chinese wedding. The tops of these tables were stacked on their sides next to the toilets, behind the highchairs and bulk plastic containers of peanut oil. On Sundays our family would eat dim sum there, mainly because there was no queuing like at other restaurants.

'Chinese people act like the food is free!' my mother would mutter, as if she wasn't one herself.

I remember the fluffy white barbecue pork buns, larger than my hand. Inside The Prosperous Red Phoenix we felt like we had slipped back home via a gaudy portal. Inside, I ate chicken feet and squid tentacles and pickled

The Prosperous Red Phoenix Restaurant

jelly fish and felt emboldened to show my true self to the kids at school. Outside the restaurant though, I recoiled at what my mother had packed for my first day—fried rice, an oyster sauce omelette and the fried-up chicken wings the butcher was selling as dog scraps. I pretended I had no lunch.

The first time The Prosperous Red Phoenix burnt down, the owner suspected a cooker accidentally left on, an electrical wiring fault. But the entire place looked like it had been blown up. The police came to investigate. By then, I was attending regular ESL classes and my English was better. But when I approached the other children in the schoolyard, they stopped talking and turned away. I caught snippets of *firebombed* and *terrorism*. I didn't know what either meant.

The second time, there was no mistaking. Then the third. My father remained silent, which was not a difficult feat as he was a traditional Chinese man. My mother gossiped within the migrant community and looked too angry to meddle with, my little sister and I careful not to get under her feet or within the reaches of her chicken-feather duster with its hard bamboo end. During a night of Mahjong playing, there was more talking among the adults. I looked at the playing tiles and found it difficult to recall the Chinese letters. That's when I knew I was losing my culture.

I cried. In fits of rage, I demanded to know why I was brought here. I was a child. I had *no choice*. My parents' faces were hard and stoic. The front of The Prosperous Red Phoenix was black around the edges.

When the restaurant reopened once again, the Chinese community rallied. Not through held banners or marching or shouted words through megaphones, but by patronage and bottoms on seats and eating and more eating. Day and night. Night after night. We fought with our stomachs. By the end of the week, I was thoroughly sick of Chinese food. I wanted Maccas.

Through the rest of my childhood, my university days and into my adulthood, The Prosperous Red Phoenix stood through times of fluctuating palates and tastes, never changing much. It still brought in the oldies for lunch.

Now in my forties, I happened to be driving in my old neighbourhood. There, along the highway, was a sign that read *For Lease*. The restaurant was abandoned.

The demise of the restaurant wasn't the sustained hatred against Chinese migrants, flaring up once every decade or so, but Covid-19. The restaurant simply could not cope without customers.

Out of interest, I googled The Prosperous Red Phoenix. Articles popped up, pertaining to the *forgotten attacks on Perth Restaurants in 1988*. But none of it is forgotten. I remember it like it was yesterday, when I first stepped foot into this country that smelt like it had been burning for a long time. Like the restaurant, the damage on me is also around the edges.

Dust and Ashes

Grace Juniper Goodwin

Geoffy was everything I thought a good man was meant to be. A strong man. A caring man. A man whose hands stayed steady when pushing a piece of thick jarrah through the bandsaw, as burnt orange dust covered the vicinity like freshly fallen snow. I can still hear the high-pitched whine of timber being cut, and the relief when the saw slowed to a stop. I used to write 'Gracie' with my pointer finger through the powdered veneer to expose the workbench, a love heart above the 'i'. If I hadn't done so, the dust might have stayed there for weeks or months completely untouched.

It seems funny now, that this bothered me. I recall deposits of hardened wood glue on the benchtops, glossy and wet-looking. Another novelty to poke and check if any were still tacky. Despite these small areas of the space that made sense to me, Geoffy's workshop remained a mystery for many years. He would go in there for hours on end, sanding and varnishing long heavy tables or shaping chopping boards with iron handles. I never actually took notice of the process from start to finish. Furniture that had been laboured over for months would come out of that workshop and be sold to eager collectors. To me it was magic.

When I reflect now on Geoffy's time in that dust-coated room producing beautiful things, I can see how being in there brought him peace. He was not an antisocial or timid man, but it was important for him to have time alone. Time to reflect. My wonderment of the workshop makes more sense now too, it was a room that embodied my grandfather's masculinity. Perhaps it was because he was so mesmerising to watch. Other times he would sit on the terrace and gaze along the river while it changed colour in the late afternoon. Very little would be said if it were he and I sitting there. It seemed unnecessary to converse when the view said it all. He always looked fascinated while looking at the river, and when he spoke it was to profess his deep gratitude for life.

I am sitting on a mossy boulder near the river, as my family take turns reaching into the deep bowl that holds the soft white ash which is Geoffy now. The young boys are excitable, their whole hands are covered in the powder as they throw it into the air before them. We laugh and clap and take photos and film slow-motion videos to try to ensure not an ounce of the experience is lost. It's my mother's turn and she wades out to a rock that has breached the water's surface, the bowl in her hands. After glancing towards us she gathers a handful and counts, 'One. Two. Three!' The ash disperses and forms into a moving cloud, it catches in the breeze and drifts slowly down the bank. I observe as my mother watches the cloud of her father disperse over the Blackwood. She takes a breath then steps off the rock and into water, presenting the bowl for my turn.

I look down at the chalky dust and think about the ridiculousness of it all. I know it's supposed to be meaningful and cathartic and an exercise of letting go, literally and metaphorically, but I can't help hearing Geoffy chuckling in my head. I can hear him saying something like, *'It might not even be me in there, who knows what happens in the crematorium.'* He was an atheist and never lived in fear of death or what happened after. This was for us. For Susie. I try to stop being logical and put my hand into the bowl, into the dust of what may or may not be my grandfather's remains. When I throw the white cloud up, it carries down the river again but this time it catches a current of air and floats on.

Frenchman Bay My Father, Frenchman Bay My Mother

Kaylee McIntyre

We stood outside the chain-link fence and watched the carcass shudder along the concrete ramp, up and up to what they call the flensing deck. The creature's skin was dark like the depths of the sea. When the men's curved tools bit into it, the outer layer of whale peeled back like a grey and white banana, the flesh inside a crimson bruise. The stench was incredible.

My father watched, transfixed. We had been here before. My father said that once upon a time he had worked on the Cheynes whalers that delivered their catch to Frenchman Bay.

This may or may not have been true.

My father said that he painted the top of the Wagin radio mast, and that his voice was the first to be transmitted from that tower. But the tower began broadcasting in 1936 and my father only arrived in Western Australia after World War II. When my father came to this country, he told everyone his name was 'Spencer'. That was a lie. When my father soon after married an Australian woman, he never mentioned his wife and young sons back in England. This was a lie of omission.

Frenchman Bay My Father, Frenchman Bay My Mother

When my father said he worked on the whale chasers, I pictured him younger, slimmer, darker-haired, braced at the bow of a ship, manning a harpoon. After all, what else does one do upon a whaling vessel? He may have scrubbed the decks. He may have been the cook. He may have cleaned the toilets. He may have spent five minutes onboard or none at all. Anyway, here we stood, and watched. It was hot. I tried to breathe through my mouth.

The engine that powered the saw carving apart the flesh drove a constant juddering roar. Seagulls screamed for scraps. The greasy miasma of rendering blubber coated our hair, our clothes, our eyes, our tongues.

Surely, we had watched for long enough now, hadn't we? We'd paid our homage, either to the men who plied their trade on the wild seas off this coast or to the dead whale.

The dismantling continued. Rip. Chop. Hack. Saw. The body was now a collection of chunks, offal and oil. The noise and smell went on. One man hosed the blood down the deck and the sloping cement, sending it back to the sea.

* * *

We scuffed along impossibly white sand, my mother and I, pretending to be shipwrecked sailors. Would we ever find rescue? If we made the rocky headland that bound Frenchman Bay, perchance we would discover civilisation beyond. The Southern Ocean tickled our feet, beckoning us with myriad shades of blue. Fooled, we ventured out until ocean tumbled bare knees.

'Too cold!' we laughed and returned to our trudge along the beach. If you hit the sand in just the right way, every footstep would squeak.

Squeak, squeak, our search for salvation continued.

My younger brothers scampered around us, squealing with delight at the warm clutch of the sand and the icy touch of the sea. Fresh salt air kissed our faces.

Squeak, squeak, trudge, trudge. Lost sailors in a lost land. Surely deliverance was around the bend.

Fortune smiled on us—a spring of fresh water cut the beach. Sweaty hands cupped, we scooped mouthfuls of clean clear water, wiped damp faces and continued our trek.

I can't recall our conversation, but I know my mother listened to my childish opinions with interest and respect, whether I discussed school, a television programme I had seen, or the weather. No topic was above or beneath her consideration.

The breeze sighed through weeping peppermint trees. Picnickers chattered. Children laughed. Seagulls squawked, riding the winds.

Frenchman Bay My Father, Frenchman Bay My Mother

We jumped—jump! jump!—looking over our shoulders at the marks we left in the sand. We were here! Ocean crept in and tidied the mess we had made. Grains of sparkling beach clung to our feet and wedged between toes.

On and on, the ragged castaways jumped and scuffed to the heaped grey boulders that marked the terminus of the bay. Children there scrambled over pitted rocks. At the bottom of shallow pools lay tiny, variegated shells and delicate ribbons of seaweed. The ocean heaved and crashed and swirled about us.

Intrepid, we explored and catalogued our discoveries, water cool and granite warm under our fingers. Waves rolled in and away, under a brilliant, unceasing sun.

Would we ever be saved?

Maybe this was our life, now.

Summer Days

Rachel McEleney

I don't remember if the sky was blue or grey, but it must've been a warm summer's day. A rare occurrence in Ireland. Ash trees formed a barrier and tall grass waved its seeded head, safe from the slasher, the hay tedder and the baler. We sat in the long grass, a circle of friends, hidden from the world. Out came the homemade wine. Fiona's creation. She didn't give it to us, we had to pay her: 50p. It wasn't worth it. Not sure what the contents were, but not grape. *Dandelion and ginger,* she said. No one wanted a second swig, but we'd paid money for the foulness. Soon the empty bottle was discarded, and we lay watching the clouds meander across the sky; like us, they were in no rush to go anywhere. The afternoon sea breeze carried a coolness with it, and we turned for home, hungry and tired. I pulled a seedhead, filling my hand with fluffy seeds and threw them into the sky. They caught on the wind and were carried off to new places, dispersed like we soon would be too.

Saaptiya?

Melanie Hobbs

Saaptiya = Have you eaten?
Kulichitiya = Have you showered?
Engevahdah = Come here.
Podah = Go away.

I don't speak it, but I know enough Tamil to understand what Thatha means most of the time. Not that he speaks to me often.

He has diabetes, like most of my elderly relatives. But unlike them, he actually takes his diet seriously. He never eats sweets, white rice or white bread, and my aunty cooks special food for him that no one else seems to want to eat. He drinks water from tall glasses and if you happen to walk past him while he is doing so, he will urge you to do the same.

Thatha is strict with his diet and strict with us. Quick to growl at us for staying up late, laughing too loudly or growing our hair too long. But he always cuts up fruit for us, and he always picks the nuts and sultanas out of his muesli to give to us. He even busts out the English here: 'Eat.'

One day, at lunch, Thatha is helping himself to some spinach to go with his black rice. Some spinach lands in his glass of water. I watch the ribbons dance like seaweed in the tall glass. No one has noticed. I want to say something, but I don't even know how. I know that the word for spinach is *kiereh* and the word for water is *thani* but I don't know how to say *Thatha, some spinach appears to have landed in your water*. I never address Thatha first. There are all these changes to the language when you're speaking to your grandfather or anyone from that generation. For instance, I can't just walk up to him and say something like *saaptiya*, to make conversation. That would be seen as incredibly rude. I'm supposed to say something like *saaptingla*. Tamil is complicated. In any case, I'm likely to be told off as soon as I open my mouth for talking when I'm supposed to be eating. So, in the end I just watch and wait, transfixed by the ribbons of spinach settling into a blob at the bottom of Thatha's glass.

Eventually, he picks up his glass, raises it to his lips, sees all this green stuff and says,

'Huh?

I can't help myself, it's too funny. I start to laugh. Thatha looks at me. But I'm not in trouble. He gives me a bright white smile and begins to laugh as well. The rest of the family are looking at us puzzled. The two of us, just for this moment, actually understand one another.

Hunger Games

Martin Lindsay

Heaven for an eleven-year-old boy was up a wood-panelled stairwell to the spacious function room at the back of the Vic Hotel.

There, beyond the white-clothed tables, was the bounty of the gods: a mid-1980s smorgasbord. A long table laden with a cornucopia of serving dishes, vats of soup, and long platters of meats and salads.

But the prize above all was the armada of prawn cocktails. A healthy portion of small pink crustaceans on a bed of lettuce in faux crystal glasses, drenched in thick Thousand Island dressing. Each accompanied by a small cocktail fork—the mark of true fine dining. I managed thirteen on my first visit, encouraged by plaudits for my ability to put them away.

Dad, dressed in the finer of his two 'going out' shirts, topped up his glass from the cask of Ben Ean Moselle that accompanied most Saturday evening dining expeditions.

Every fifteen minutes, the true miracle of the smorgasbord was bestowed: empty dishes replaced with new platters or refilled to their full splendour. And another platoon of prawn cocktails, despite us having long since moved from entrees to mains.

We had my twelfth birthday at The Vic, if simply to prove to my best mate Brendon that I wasn't lying about the culinary bonanza on offer.

We went bloody nuts.

By the end of the night, the record stood with me: Twenty-two prawn cocktails along with multiple plates loaded with food. Guinness Records should have been notified if just for the possibility of 'Youngest Person to Develop Gout.' Bloated and belly-sore, we eventually rolled out, unsure if we would see thirteen.

Luckily, when I did, a Pizza Hut franchisee had arrived in town. Foolishly, they offered All-You-Can-Eat Wednesdays in a town that proved to be ravenously hungry. From then on, many birthdays happened to fall on a Wednesday—earning a free ice cream cake with sparklers—no matter what truth calendars might reveal.

School groups would descend like locust plagues, devouring the conveyor line of piping hot pizzas. Intense alpha-male competitions ensued to cram down the most pieces—thick crust, no less. Thin and crispy effectively conceded cowardice and inferior stomach capacity. Woe betide bystanders if different school groups coincided. The delivery of a fresh platter spurred a rush to the self-serve area, triangular pizza knives wielded in territorial dominance like a polysaturated *West Side Story*.

We felt no guilt. This was the 1980s, where greed was good. Excess was actively encouraged. This was the generation that hair-lacquered a hole in the ozone layer. We ate all we could and more, hesitating only to puke in

Hunger Games

their garden as we departed, like binge-sated Romans at Saturnalia.

The Pizza Hut is now a car wash, a coincidental metaphor for their reckless business model washed down the drain.

The Vic's smorgasbord nights ended, followed by the closure of the restaurant section, then the entire pub itself. Perhaps their happy hours were too joyous. Finally, The Vic was knocked down for a new development that never quite happened. It remains a strange cavity on Marine Terrace, lined with rubble, as though left as a lesson by a self-righteous dentist of the dangers of excess.

Now, in my older, wiser age of calorie counting and disappointing daily weigh-ins, the mere memory stacks on two kilograms. If I told my doctor of my capacious exploits, she'd have a heart attack quicker than any cholesterol reading she might warn me of.

On rare occasion, I see prawn cocktails on a restaurant menu and the old instincts kick in—the stomach rumbles, the mouth salivates, the pulse increases. But maybe that's just high blood pressure? So, now I apply discipline, turn past the entrees, and look for low-carb options.

We still pay for the consequences of that greedy age. We only find out after we've eaten all we can.

Beach Body

Asha Burnett

It's summer. It's the middle of January, in the hottest part of the day. I'm driving home from the beach. My hair is crunchy and matted. A weird sheen of salt water, sweat and sunscreen coats my skin, a perpetually sticky lacquer that never dries.

Swinging my car into the driveway, I push it into park and wrench up the hand break. The backs of my thighs burn as they rip away from the car seat, the coarse fabric irritating my already sunburnt skin. In a hurry to unlock the door, I drop my keys and have to bend over to grab them; bags and towels and clothes are haphazardly draped over me like I'm some kind of pack mule.

I'm through the door, but there's still that awkward shuffle down the hall to my bedroom before I can drop my shit and head to the bathroom. My temples throb with pain.

In the bathroom I peel off my lukewarm bathers, still damp and clinging to my skin. Hidden pockets of sand fall to the floor. I step under the showerhead and gasp.

Crisp, cool, clean water rushes over me. I feel the grime of day slip from my skin—I watch it swirl down

Beach Body

the drain. The tangles in my hair begin to loosen as I let the knots of my mind slowly unravel.

I should not care if they saw the rolls of my stomach as I bent for my towel. If they spotted the thin line of blonde hairs on my shin that I missed with the razor. Noted the peeling skin on my shoulder blades as my friend applied sunscreen to my back. Glimpsed the slight shaving rash on my bikini line, how the ties of my bather bottoms dug into my hips, the pimple on my chin, my split ends, my weird tan lines, the scar on my side.

I try and let the thrum of the water hitting the shower floor drown out the insecurities that stifle me. The fresh water soothes my heated skin, but not the redness in my cheeks.

The Gym Horse

Sean Murphy

Dark clouds signal a coming storm. Class Nine Blue swelters in rising humidity. About forty boys are shirtless in the early summer heat.

A gym horse, surrounded by rough hessian bags filled with foam rubber, and a home-made wooden springboard beckon. The excitement is palpable. The boys at this suburban Perth Catholic high school have never had equipment like this for their weekly phys ed class.

Mr Harvard is a maths teacher but also a superb gymnast. He has a strong, tight body and he knows it. His groomed beard and blond locks betray a vanity that takes time before a mirror to honour.

'Ghent. On the horse, now,' he bellows.

Mitchell Ghent is overweight and routinely mocked. He is mostly good humoured but has a well-known temper.

He climbs awkwardly onto the horse, ruddy faced, more from the heat and embarrassment than any anger.

'Feet over the front, bend forward,' Mr Harvard positions Ghent on top of the horse. He marks out ten steps from the springboard, sprints and glides effortlessly

The Gym Horse

over Ghent. His legs splay outward in a half split as his palms lightly touch the student's back.

'Class. Line up now.' The teacher's military-like demeanour would normally attract some teenage impudence and defiance, but no one wants to miss a jump on the springboard.

The usual alpha males push and shove at the head of a ragged queue, eager to show off their physical prowess. Barton Farmer is the toughest kid in year nine. He takes his place at the front of the line without challenge. He runs in heavily and soars over Ghent, slapping his two palms hard on the hapless student's bare back.

Ghent yelps in pain.

Bill Seward follows up and also slaps down hard on Ghent's back.

'I will fucking kill you, Seward.'

Mr Harvard smirks but says nothing.

The class bullies are enlivened like a pride of lions sharing a kill. The first five jumpers all smack Ghent hard. He is seriously wound up. With each hit he cries out, naming the perpetrator and threatening revenge.

'Okay, that's enough you lot,' Mr Harvard says. 'Right. Cartwright. Get up there. Ghent, back of the line.'

Cartwright mutters inaudibly, but it's obvious he's saying *fuck you, Harvard.*

'Alright, the first one to slap Cartwright will be on the horse. I'll give the entire class free reign to hit you as hard as they want.'

Ghent walks to the rear fuming with anger but his back looks angrier. There's a massive red welt between his shoulder blades.

No one slaps Cartwright.

Mick O'Brien waits anxiously, more worried about Mr Harvard's threat than enjoying the springboard and bouncy bags.

He takes his turn, hits the timber board sweetly and barely touches Cartwright. He bounces on the hessian bags and rolls to the grass below. In his relief he doesn't hear Cartwright cry out in fake pain.

'Right, O'Brien, I warned you,' Mr Harvard's smirk returns.

'Get down, Cartwright. You can have first slap.'

For O'Brien resistance is futile. As a pre-pubescent fourteen-year-old he has no power, no voice and no hope. He begs anyway.

'Mr Harvard, he's lying. I barely touched him. He's lying.'

Cartwright can't believe his good fortune. O'Brien called him out for stealing his school jumper earlier in the year. He was forced to take it off in class, revealing O'Brien's name on the collar tag.

'You deserve this, O'Brien,' Cartwright says more to the class than to O'Brien. He runs in, hits the springboard hard and hits O'Brien's back harder.

Farmer and the other bullies push their way to the top of the queue and eagerly join the cruelty-fest. Even

The Gym Horse

normally mild-mannered students are emboldened by the invitation to violence.

Mr Harvard watches silently, unmoved by O'Brien's tears of pain and frustration.

'Mr Harvard, this is wrong.'

The excited chatter and cheering stop. Jack Keenan stands defiantly between the class and the gym horse. He is not the biggest boy in Nine Blue but he has form as a fighter. No one moves.

'This is too much.' He helps O'Brien down. Snot, saliva and tears congeal on the boy's face and in his hair. A barely audible *thank you* emerges from deep in his throat.

Mr Harvard says nothing.

Half a century later, that day still stings. The truth is, I am Mick O'Brien, but it's less painful to tell the story as an observer. Jack Keenan (name also changed) is a lifelong friend.

Grounds for Dismissal

Susan Midalia

On 14 October 1968, at precisely 10:59 am, the wheatbelt town of Meckering in Western Australia experienced a severe earthquake. It lasted 40 seconds and measured 6.9 on the Richter Scale. Townspeople later reported hearing a prolonged ominous rumbling, followed by what they thought was a deafening clap of thunder. Then they saw the earth swell and heave and buckle. People ran screaming from their fragile houses.

There were no fatalities, although some twenty-eight people incurred injuries.

In Perth, the capital city of Western Australia, located 130 kilometres from Meckering, the earth barely trembled, chandeliers merely tinkled, a few bricks were dislodged, and I lost my virginity at the age of seventeen.

The next morning, when I heard about the earthquake, I was both grateful there had been no loss of life and thrilled by the knowledge that the earth had split asunder, shattering our arrogant assumption of mastery over nature. But when the boy lying beside me asked, with a glint in his dark blue eyes, if the earth had moved for me, I shot him a look of contempt.

Grounds for Dismissal

    I told him that the earthquake had a maximum Mercalli intensity of IX.

    He didn't know what I was talking about, and as he grabbed for my breast again, he didn't seem to care.

Years later, in bed with an intelligent, cultured man, I told him how I'd lost my virginity. I said the boy wasn't interested in the wonder of an earthquake, or in the science that measured its astonishing strength. The man reached out to embrace me, then whispered in my ear that maximum Mercalli intensity was classified as Violent. Then he released me from his arms, grabbed my breast and told me that he really liked it violent. Knowing I could make the earth move all by myself, I calmly put on my clothes and walked out the door.

Hutt Lagoon, Pink Lake

Jay Chesters

'It's a long drive to dispose of a body,' Kate says, and I jump at her voice.

'Sorry, my bad.'

'You're OK. I was … somewhere else.'

I don't know where I was. I was lost in the years, lost in memories of my own.

'I know. But we're *here*, Hutt Lagoon.'

Kate does this thing where you can almost hear the capital letters when she speaks. It's quite a talent.

'It sounds like something from Star Wars,' I reply.

Kate smiles, 'Grandpa loved this place.'

I haven't seen the pink lake in years, and I'd forgotten it was so vibrant. I didn't know anything could feel that way anymore.

'Come on, we have miles to go before we sleep.' Kate gestures to the silver urn at her feet and she softly touches my hand.

'Time to go, Grandpa,' I agree. 'Before someone sees us.'

The Bluest Skies

Alison Middleton

Where I'm from, the beach curves around, mimicking the shape of the crescent moon. Only locals know about this place; you won't find any tourists here. It's a ten-minute drive off the main road then another couple of miles along a private farm track that is unforgiving to a car's suspension.

Everyone else comes here in summer. But for me, this beach in winter is my happy place. I welcome the crisp, clean air and windburn that's cold enough to buffer both skin and mind.

We scramble down the dunes to walk arm in arm along the hard, compacted wet sand. I take my first full breath in a long, long time and it feels like the fresh salt air leaps right into my lungs.

I know it's possible to be homesick for both a place and a person. To have both in the same moment feels like the best kind of gluttony. Over more than twenty years of friendship this woman has been my rock, tethering me to home while I live my life in the most isolated big city in the world.

The skies in Angus are at their brightest blue in the coldest winter. Here, at Lunan Bay, the skies contrast with the darkest blue ink where the North Sea meets the horizon.

We walk, nodding to a lone dog walker, smiling at the golden retriever running into the shock of the cold water. It seems like the more the sun shines, the colder it is.

Every time I'm home we come here to the empty beach which stretches out before us, following the lines revealed at low tide. We walk until we reach the medieval Red Castle, which was built by King William the Lion to repel Viking invasions in the twelfth century.

Local rumour has it that Robert the Bruce once stayed here. The red sandstone ruin stands high on a bluff overlooking the beach and sea. It looks set to crumble but stands resilient in the face of the elements.

She squeezes my arm. We both know how that feels.

Bees

K. T. Downs

Our father kept bees. The hives were the square, timber box sort, painted white, that stacked on top of each other. He had two stacks of two. I thought they looked like apartment blocks—which were something I'd only read about.

The bees were there to pollinate the citrus trees. The hives sat solidly in their stacks in a quiet little grassy patch between our packing shed and the homemade orchard gate.

The grassy patch was there because it contained a disused mine shaft, which had become a well in my grandfather's time, and was now in the process of being filled with farm debris, such as old fencing.

The position of the old mine shaft made the bees a double hazard. We were doubly forbidden from going near them.

The hives came from our farming cousins at Oakabella. They took their bees seriously, moving them around on the old green Bedford truck, to feast on paddocks of Paterson's curse, then later in the year, on eucalyptus stands. I thought a truckload of bee hives was one of the most picturesque sights in our district.

Little colonies of white hives appeared just behind roadside vegetation, or even in our own paddocks for a few weeks, and then moved away again, like gypsies. I was a dreamy child, and wondered if our bees wished they could go too.

Our cousins had a proper setup in a shed for processing their honey, then selling it to shops. In those days we bought our milk powdered, in one-kilo tins. For retail sales new tins were bought in bulk, but in our large extended family, there was always a refill and a swap being enacted—pie melons for citrus, honey for marmalade, jars for tins.

Dad's bees had a very settled life by the orchard gate, in reach of blossom all year. It was not a commercial operation. The bee numbers built up slowly, and we were not processing honey very often. When the hive was getting full and the bees needed more space, it was a family affair to extract the waxy frames and drain the golden gift inside.

Dad never bought a thing he could make.

The extractor was made from an old washing machine tub, with a welded frame holder working from the fixture that normally held the agitator, and a handle attached on the outside to gently turn it. Dad had a special blade for slicing off the waxy coating over the honeycomb, down the length of the thin frame. We spun it slowly in turn until our shoulders hurt, and all of the honey was in the container below the frame. The whole process took place at the hives and in the laundry.

Bees

Our father wore clean, white overalls to rob the bees—for hygiene I think, or maybe it was easier to see where the bees were. He wore a dark net hat covering his face and shoulders. It was not long after the moon landing that Dad first robbed the bees, with me in attendance holding and passing things as needed—matches, gloves, smoker—I thought he looked like an astronaut.

Rags were lit and quickly covered to deny air. The handle was a kind of squeeze box. Each squeeze blew a puff of smoke from the smouldering rags.

He lifted the top off the box, puffing smoke from his hand-held smoker at every step, to keep the bees sleepy, until the whole lid was lifted and gently placed on the ground. We never took out all of the frames, and we never took our eyes off them while they were being lifted. Things unravelled pretty quickly if the smoker failed.

En plein air paintings, with any sign of produce or a smudgy hive—like those of the Heidelberg School—take me straight back to the company of our strong, patient dad in white overalls, giving us a go on all the different devices he made and used.

How sad I feel in the supermarket to find honey has an ingredients list, including rice syrup. That even natural honey may be from bees fed sugar water. That bees are considered a threatened species.

I don't think a child could have looked up to a man more than I looked up to Dad, in his astronaut whites, controlling fire in one hand and frames of honeycomb crawling with stinging bees, in the other.

They Watch

Miriam Fisher

It's late. I leave my friends at the bar, shaking away their offers to drop me home. I will stick to the well-lit streets where the tuktuks run, I tell them, as I've done scores of times before.

But as the tuktuks thin out, the lure of the narrow shortcut that winds its way to my door is too great. I glance around then turn down the alley, quickening my pace.

Night outside Kathmandu Valley is a glittering dome of strobing stars, but inside it the pollution herniating the sky snuffs them out, with rolling blackouts plunging the city into pitch. The labyrinthine streets will remain muted in dust until the monsoon arrives to scour them clean again.

The streetlights wink out as I look at my watch. Load shedding has started early.

The alley is flanked by high, bending bricked walls topped with glossy shards of glass to deter thieves. Familiarity dissolves at night, when shadows alter dimensions and draw those walls in tighter. I count my steps, a human metronome ticking towards home.

They Watch

I stop, peering back into the darkness. I hear the distant beeping of traffic on the ring road that encircles the city, and the rumble of the affluent starting up their generators. There are two bends to go.

I stop again. My ears burn in the darkness, the hairs at their opening bristling as they probe the air.

There.

Soft and then louder, more insistent. I run. The night brightens and dulls, brightens and dulls as blood floods my eyes with each knocking pulse.

One more bend. The gate is locked after dark and the uneasy logistics of scaling it at speed flicker through my mind. My assailant closes in.

A pixelated blur emerges from the gloom ahead and rushes at my face. *The fuck is that?* I wince but no impact comes.

A guttural snarl tears a hole in the thick air and disappears into the scramble at my heel. I reach for the top of the gate and launch myself up and over, landing awkwardly on the broken stoop, keys clanging against the prayer bowl as they slip from my fingers.

The gate rattles violently as weight slams against it. Landlord-dai has forgotten the padlock. I fumble desperately for the keys as the gate crashes against its loose hinges again and again.

I am inside, bolting the door behind me. My heart beats out the sounds of the rabid melee that boils into the darkness.

Miriam Fisher

I wake to the chorus of morning puja bells and gingerly open the gate. The night's only proof is congealed in the darkened dust at my feet. A tan bitch sits on her left hip, a leathery apron of nipples draped over her legs. She regards me with her silent golden eyes before trotting up to the chowk where the street dogs have gathered for the day, taking their places as the neighbourhood slowly awakens.

They watch.

I Woke Before Dawn Thinking of Wagin

Donna Mazza

The first time I went to Wagin was to pick up a 1948 Velocette motorcycle for my absent brother, who had bought it online. My beloved drove with a car-trailer through the town's faded glory in the middle of a silent weekday. It was dry-ice cold.

The seller's house was flaky asbestos; low corrugated shed scummed with engine oil facing the wide street. Multiples of railway tracks the other side. He wanted to talk about the Ford Fairlane in his shed. Starved for company. Scar on his head looked like a bashing.

Perched on the A-frame of the trailer, I was bone cold, watching corellas eat fallen gumnuts between the railway lines. I accidentally mentioned an Italian car we used to have, just to remind them I was there. There followed a longwinded story of a mechanic we all knew. My beloved gave me an eyeroll. Then Velocette-man overshared confessions of his heyday in organised crime, which led me to think Wagin was self-enforced witness protection.

For a vegetarian, there are always paltry lunch options in small towns, but in Wagin there wasn't even a bakery open. Ironic considering where wheat grows.

Only options were the supermarket or the servo outside town, which was obviously a truck stop for drivers whose destination was not Wagin. With hot chips and coffee, we drove home to the coast, talking through the true crime stories we'd just heard.

The drive was pastoral-picturesque with flocks of sheep and creek beds twisting between granite outcrops. Patches of struggling trees. No sign of a grand river which might sweep someone away. Dead rabbits on the verge but no dead kangaroos as there are down south, or dead eagles as there are up north. Long driveways led to faraway homesteads.

The earth was cut into neat shapes: fenced and deforested. Yellow quadrants of rapeseed. Words hold truths that history tries to deny, and in Australia we call it canola for a reason. This landscape is grim evidence of pillaging: a cleared paradise so massive that the brownout can be seen from Richard Branson's rocket ship. I've read that the scar of the Wheatbelt is the size of England.

We stopped at Wellington Dam on the way home. It was overflowing a fine lacework of salty water. I already wanted to go back to Wagin. We hadn't really scratched the surface.

* * *

We return a couple of winters later with our daughters and dog. This time we stop at the giant ram and stand under its huge, concrete testicles for a photo shoot. There

I Woke Before Dawn Thinking of Wagin

is something darkly symbolic about petrified testicles in a place like this.

In the Wetlands Park beside the ram, there is no wet land. A church group is wearing matching t-shirts and having a picnic. They line up with red parasols and sing in a language I don't understand. It's the most humans I have seen in Wagin and I wonder what their roots are, these people on the dry wetland. I realise that if you add an A onto the end of Wagin, it is Wagina. I find this hard to reconcile with the concrete testicles and rapeseed.

The emporium where I might have found a delightful treasure has closed down. We buy ingredients from the supermarket and try to find a nice spot for a picnic at the back of a lake that is just a wide arena of damp mud. A lone teenager is riding a horse through the scrubby tracks. She doesn't look at us. On the tailgate of the car I make salad wraps while the kids take photos of the dog. It's a broad panorama. When there is something to focus on, the subject looks better here than it does in other places. The light and the sparse landscape highlight life and colour.

Amid low branches, bright golden lichen like a shade of eighties laminex, specked with grey-green curds is slow-growing in the windless chill. The white sky of low clouds makes everything shimmer and glow. A ragged fringe of dead trees drop piece-by-piece into the lakebed.

It wasn't an ideal place for a picnic. Someone with a trailer drives past and stares at us murderously and I snare my long skirt on a spiky bush.

The dog and my daughter are the screensaver on my phone, frozen in Wagin. It's a couple of years since it was taken, and I said at the time we had seen enough and I never wanted to return. But today I woke before dawn thinking of Wagin.

Exhalation

Ellen O'Brien

The highway is deafening. It even drowns out the ocean, to a degree. It's sure to be hot this week, but this morning I sit in a long-sleeved rashie, wrapped in the red tartan rug while my green tea cools rapidly on the table. On the veranda, the chairs are all tied together in a congenial, teatime raft. I'd had to clamber in between the old fishing rope, more fray than wax now. There's still a risk that the wind will blow them away, even though winter is over.

There is something about the smell of the house this morning, perhaps all the more striking after my absence of a few weeks. As I was rummaging for a jumper (all gone now—hence the rug) the gentle scent of her wardrobe enveloped me. Strange how a scent can linger or loiter, clinging to places of long association. The walnut wood still smells of the hat boxes, elbow-length gloves and Oroton handbags that had nestled there since the 1960s.

Even the garden, recently drenched by the reticulation, seems to be giving up its secrets. The ground exudes the vapour of boat fuel. At least, I think it is boat fuel—it could be the result of one cousin's haphazard mechanics in the now-empty garage. Below that, a faint note of fish, of the sea, as though years of gutted catches are breathing out at last.

By the time I finish writing, my tea is completely cold. The edges of the tartan rug are damp with dew or seawater, and the highway has settled into its mid-morning rhythm. In the silences between sporadic motorists, the sea gapes large. Together, the house and I listen.

Shattered Expectations

Chrissie Horley

I was so excited to share the news with my mum. This was something I knew I had always wanted, and it had happened sooner than I thought it might. How she would react wasn't certain, of course, but I was hopeful she would be excited too. She answered the phone.

'Hi Mum, it's me. I have some news to tell you,' I paused. 'You're going to be a grandmother!' the excitement evident in my voice. 'I'm pregnant!'

Silence.

'Oh,' she said after a few seconds, the strain in her voice obvious. 'Can I ask, was it planned?'

Transgression

Rashida Murphy

The books on my shelves are my familiars. In my nightmares, I have the same feeling of helplessness at their loss as I do when dreaming of losing people I love. *Lolita* lives on my bookshelf, despite my horror, to remind me that lyrical writing about paedophilia can still teach me a thing or two about sentence structure. Plath and Hughes inhabit the same literary universe and, as poets, sit side by side, but I mutter 'wife-killer' every time I pass Hughes on the bookshelf. I stroke Sylvia's spine and move her away from the blue-jacketed copy of *Birthday Letters*.

My Indian grandfather, a venerable old gent with a goatee and round-rimmed spectacles, recalled being called 'boy' by British soldiers younger than his son. Sometimes he was called 'Gunga Din' and one of my earliest acts of transgression was to tear out the first five pages of Kipling's *Collected Poems*. For this I was spanked and banned from proximity to books, an ordeal so dire I retrieved the pages, sticky taped them back, begged forgiveness and was allowed back into my father's library. Aunties with dusters watched suspiciously and hovered close in case I attacked books again.

Transgression

When an elderly relative asked if I'd read *The Far Pavilions* by M. M. Kaye, I responded by asking if she'd read Salman Rushdie. *Midnight's Children* rollicked into my life when I was twenty years old. For the first time, I saw myself in a modern novel, an urban, mixed-up young woman with multiple narratives colliding against her skin. Those familiar multilingual worlds spoke to me with an urgency none of the English writers in my father's library had been able to provide. For days afterwards I smiled and thought of the novel—the perforated sheets through which a girl's stomach may be glimpsed, Saleem Sinai's troublesome nose, and the way languages live in the worlds we imagine.

Later, as a young mum in Australia, I would attempt to recreate the chaos and multiplicity of my birth country by telling my daughter the stories I remembered. I tried to raise her with the secular expansion I was used to, but this was difficult in a monocultural, monolingual society, and I simply confused her. My fascination with Hindu, Catholic and Islamic scripture meant that I told stories of golden chariots where the charioteer was also a blue-skinned god; I elaborated on sombre descriptions of martyrs and sacrifices; I waxed lyrical over the feast days of saints. It may not have been the ideal introduction to the country of *Midnight's Children* for a child growing up in Perth. Sane friends introduced me to beloved Australian classics. Despite my efforts, my daughter showed zero interest in the adventures of Snugglepot and Cuddlepie, or in magic puddings and possums.

Guiltily, I started reading *The Children's Mahabharata* with her and she was hooked. As an independent reader she skated happily between goth, horror, classics, poetry and punk. I considered my job as a mother done.

Our grandchildren are growing up in another state. I wait for visits and the chance to read stories. Perhaps we can start with *This Is a Poem That Heals Fish*. Then I can tell them about countries where aunties with cloth dusters chase recalcitrant children around dusty libraries and where gods steal buttermilk from their mothers. I may even tell them how we knew what to expect when we heard church bells, temple bells, school bells, cow bells, rickshaw bells, anklets, toe rings, glass bangles and calls to prayer. I could tell them about the bearded Sufi who came every Friday and called out to my grandparents, who in turn called us, and we all gathered around to listen to the story of the prophet who pawned his children and magicked pearls from his wife's tears when she wept for them. The same story, every time. If I shut my eyes I can still hear him.

Or I could lead my grandchildren to my shelves and let them choose.

Brushstrokes in the Shape of Us

Alastair McLean

I have just spent forty-nine minutes naked, but this is the first time tonight I feel fully aware of my own shape. I can feel her eyes watching me from the bed.

I should've shut the door behind me, I think to myself. I flush the toilet and wash my hands fast, trying to avoid looking into the mirror that takes up most of the wall in her bathroom.

I need to get dressed. I need to be blissfully unaware of how I look. I rush to my pants; her eyes follow me across the room, wherever I go. I trip over whilst putting them on and fall to my knees beneath her.

I look up and become fully aware of her shape.

This makes me want to cover myself faster.

She looks like a Renaissance painting and I look like a Jackson Pollock.

'You're so gorgeous,' she softly says.

My face lights up and my heart begins to burn.

I don't understand how she is saying this about me.

I launch into her arms, and my wide-fit jeans fall off.

'I love you,' I say as we lay naked together, hoping she'll say it too.

Advantage Receiver

Mark Keenan

My wife doesn't remember sending the text, but I recall receiving it.

My eldest son was playing doubles on the tennis court next to where I sat. I'd moved out of the mid-March sun into the shade, but the reflected heat from the concrete playing surface still made my head throb. Maybe I shouldn't have drunk those last couple of beers. Drinking the last of my water, I stood and waited for the point to finish.

My son looked at me, checking to see if I'd seen the shot he'd made. I gave him a thumbs up. He had a good volley; at least when he moved his feet enough to get in the right position. I turned my bottle upside down, to show him it was empty, and pointed at the clubhouse to let him know I'd be back soon. He nodded and returned to his position at the net.

He was sixteen. The same age I had been when I'd played tennis in Country Week, an annual multi-sports carnival between rural high schools. I was honoured to be part of my town's team. And proud of myself too.

None of my kids took to the sport the way I had. They'd all played but then given it away. My son had

Advantage Receiver

decided to give it another go and joined a pennants team. I stopped beside the tap to watch the next point. My son's partner served but he threw the ball too low. It went in but it was slow and easily collected. The opposing receiver thumped it hard, past my son's outstretched raquet, the ball landing just inside the baseline. Game. Change ends.

I took the lid off my bottle and turned on the tap.

I wished I'd taken him to the courts more often when he was younger, like my mum had with me. She always found time for a hit-up at the club a couple of times a week.

But I had an engineering business to run, a wife and three children to care for, and a house to maintain. I attended every school athletics day and all the swim meets. I was manager or coach for every one of my kids' sports teams. My dad had never seen me hit a ball, not even when I made the town championship final. Still, I should have spent more time at the courts with him. And his brother and sister. I was doing everything I could. But it was never enough, not to me.

I replaced the lid on the bottle and took a sip.

It would be years later when I would understand why I was so hard on myself.

I needed to be a better dad than mine had been.

More than that, I needed to be perfect.

Nowadays, I live with my imperfection. And I have learned to practise self-compassion: this is a moment of suffering, suffering is a part of life, may I be kind and compassionate to myself in this moment.

The text from my wife arrived while I walked back to the shade. Lifting my sunglasses onto the top of my head and shielding the phone screen with my hand, I read it.

You are doing a wonderful job of caring for all of us. Maybe you can care for yourself and drink a bit less.

Later, at home, while my son chatted to his mum about the match, I emptied every remaining bottle of alcohol into the sink.

I have been sober now for ten years.

On the Other Side Is Antarctica

Emily Tsokos Purtill

On a beach south of Albany, close to where the ANZACs departed, I stand at the raging Southern Ocean. My phone doesn't have coverage so I can't tell you exactly which beach I am on, only that the waves here are deep, rolling, serious. On the other side is Antarctica. If my eyes could see beyond the horizon, it would be right in front of me. But I can only feel the chill from this side of the Southern Ocean, from this shore.

I have never been to Antarctica, have only had the merest of brushes with it, through images and in books. I always want to know more, imploring those with firsthand knowledge for details. I want something other than *cold*. I want there to be something else, something magical, something mythical.

This stormy beach, however, is the sort of place that you could write about for days, and yet you might only emerge with a tone that is melancholy, slightly gothic, *Rebecca*-esque. Not the red rhododendrons, but the location of the murder itself. The boathouse. But that was another coast, another continent, another ocean. This ocean, this gateway to Antarctica, is something else. The Antipodes.

I recall in Shirley Hazzard's *The Great Fire* there were two British brothers in Wellington waiting for their father, an Antarctic explorer. Helen observes them at a local dance. She is already in love with Aldred. She wonders what their 'explorer-father' had taken to read. What do people take to read in Antarctica? I would start with *The Transit of Venus*.

On this beach the clouds are very low. I could reach up and touch one, scoop it out of the sky and serve it as a dessert. I never imagine Antarctica as cloudy. In my head, there are clear blue skies and the whitest of snow. In my head it looks like a ski field, with penguins. But that is too clichéd to be real.

I find a thin pink canister of sherbet, from a town in England, lying on the sand. It is the size of my little finger. The wording is embossed on the plastic. I wonder who ate the sherbet within, how it ended up here? How many years ago? It seems quite old, like something people ate in the 1950s. I must look it up, find this sherbet factory online. Trace its path to this beach.

I read about Lego washing up on English shores from cargo ships sunk twenty-five years ago. I spend a lot of time thinking about Lego, how it will be here when we are all gone. Circling in some shape or form. It will outlast all of us. The Ninjago dragon, the Guggenheim model, the lighthouse (with flashing light accessory).

Lumps of coal from the bottom of the ocean floor wash up in Albany sometimes, from the previously coal-fired ships that are buried beneath. There are so

On the Other Side Is Antarctica

many of these ships, dormant until a snorkeler or diver finds a plank of wood, a treasure chest, a coin. So many shipwrecks, we have museums dedicated to them.

We are near Cape Vancouver. I lived in the other Vancouver, but that was twenty years ago now. This beach reminds me of that rugged Pacific Ocean coast, the islands and inlets. Wreck Beach. The tempo of the waves are the same, somehow. I think of my friends and how we used to eat salmon sushi and drink Long Island Iced Teas. It was our first experience of living away from home.

After an hour I have a canvas bag full of cerulean plastic pieces, rope, the sherbet canister. If everyone did something small, would it fix the problem? I know it's all too far gone for that. But I will always love stormy beaches like these, on the brink of somewhere colder beyond.

I wonder if we come back next year, in twenty or forty years, will our footsteps be underwater? Perhaps this will not be a beach at all. The sea higher, Antarctica further away. Not a shipwreck, but a wreck of some other kind.

Sisters

Lesley McKay

I always knew that I had three half-sisters on the other side of the world. Related by swirly DNA, the same but different. I wondered if they had the same nose, eyes, a twisted sense of humour.

Mum, *my* mum that is, not theirs, said little about them. I have some old photos of me with my dad. Least said about him the better, apparently. My favourite photo is of me in his arms as a newborn baby: I've got jet-black curly hair. He looks a nice man, but who knows really. I remember little of that time. He was a Queensland cattle auctioneer, and I recall sitting on the wooden rails of the saleyards and being impressed that he could shout out the numbers so fast and loud.

I think we can safely say that my English rose mother and Australian auctioneer dad weren't exactly compatible, and after a few inharmonious years, Mum hauled me back to England where I experienced some firsts: snow, accents I couldn't comprehend and living indoors most of the year. We moved up to Scotland where I found the language even more impenetrable and I felt a foreigner with my Aussie accent.

Sisters

By then Mum had found husband number four. She'd been widowed twice during the war before migrating to Australia as a ten-pound Pom in the 1950s.

I remember feeling not only foreign at high school in Scotland but also slightly less than adequate. My mother was advised against preparing me to go to university as I wasn't sufficiently clever. It didn't help matters that I was the only person in the school to play the flute. I was bullied and ridiculed, which I think just made me try harder. I don't remember being self-aware as a teenager but realised slowly and usefully that I was a diligent and honest person and could achieve things simply by working hard. My choice of career as an accountant surprised everyone, because it was very rare for a female at that time to start or complete the six-year training. When I phoned my mother six years later to tell her that I had indeed passed my finals and qualified, I was slightly deflated by her comment, 'Are you sure?'

Every now and then I am introduced to a new member of the wider family, a relative I never knew I had. Recently it was my middle half-sister's daughter, given up for adoption at birth, the Catholic way. She came to her mum's funeral. That's a little hard to cope with, knowing she never actually met her mum. The atmosphere between us is antarctic.

My eldest half-sister was eighteen and the youngest was eleven when I arrived, unbidden and unwanted into their world, courtesy of their new stepmother.

My youngest half-sister and I are linked now by cancer. See what DNA does?

There are many things we can never discuss, my sisters and I. It's enough, now that we're all old and living in the same country, that we can be friends. Friends with history that hurts, like the band aid was ripped off too fast.

The Back Lane

Richard Rossiter

In the end it was boredom that made the difference. Not theirs, ours. My cousin and me. One of the bossy neighbours said the back lane was a disgrace—overgrown with long, dry grass which was dangerous in the middle of summer—and untidy with bottles and stuff just lying around. So he cleaned up his section and told the others they had to do likewise. If he'd asked nicely, they probably would have been cooperative. As it was, they ignored him, told him to go away and mind his own business.

It was late summer, and I was visiting my cousin whose house was a bike ride away from where I lived. We were nine years old. There was no one home at his place and we were wondering what to do next. It was a warm afternoon and we'd already played jumping off the outdoor toilet roof, which was quite high, and jolted your feet. And we'd hidden away in a cave in the plumbago hedge between his place and the neighbours and sucked on pretend cigarettes, sections of cane surreptitiously removed from the outdoor chair which sat on his verandah.

Then he said, *Mum wanted to get rid of those newspapers that are in the baby's bath. I reckon we could burn them.*
Good idea.

So we pulled the tin bath from under the house, found a box of matches, and lit the papers. The only trouble was, they kept going out. They'd smoulder a bit on the edge and that was it. We'd left them lying flat, one on top of the other, and didn't have the wit to scrunch them up.

I think we'd better get rid of them, he said. So we tipped the bath over the back fence.

We looked at each other. *Wanna go down the swamp?* I asked.

He nodded.

At the swamp, about fifteen minutes away, we had a home-built canoe hidden at the edge. We pushed it through the tangle of reeds and sank into the mud, which stuck to our feet. Then we checked for leeches. It was hot and still, with mosquitoes endlessly buzzing around and landing when they got a chance to suck your blood. There were lots of dead trees in the middle and a few water birds. We didn't see any other people and didn't expect to. As we paddled, we waited for something to happen.

After a while we left the water and spent some time in the giant mulberry tree that grew nearby. We had sense enough to take our shirts off and the juice dribbled down our bare bodies. It looked like war paint.

The Back Lane

We walked back slowly, with no idea what to do next. As we turned the corner into his street, we saw people standing around further down and then the sound of a fire engine blaring its siren. It swept around the corner and pulled up at the back lane. Then we noticed it—the smoke.

We ran the rest of the way and saw that the fire had already burnt quite a lot of the wild oats and was pushing up against the timber fences. It didn't take long for the firemen to start pumping water and the flames began to die down.

I looked at my cousin.

He just stared ahead and didn't say anything.

God … we did it! That newspaper … but I thought it was out.

Yeah, he said.

A little later, one of the firemen walked up to us. *Did you kids see anything, know how it started?*

Nup. We weren't here, said my cousin.

We were down the swamp, I added.

From then on, that was the best kept lane in the district; some people had flowers growing against the fences. It was neat, tidy, raked over. Not a glimpse of wild oats. Eventually it was paved like so many others and order prevailed. The grumpy neighbours talked pleasantly to the bossy one. Much of the swamp remained, except it became a lake.

After that day at the end of summer, we didn't go down to the swamp very often. Maybe that was the last time. And I don't remember jumping off the toilet again, either—with my arms held out, as if I were flying.

Don't Oversell It

Shannon Farrelly

'Maybe it's a water park?' Erica suggests to her siblings, as they squirm behind her in their car seats.

'Yeah, park!' My youngest, Nellie, swings her little legs, tapping out a rhythm with her heels on the sticky upholstery.

I laugh and change lanes to escape the learner driver ahead of us, then steal a glance in my rear-view mirror.

Behind me, my son's face tracks the scenery passing his window. His voice is hopeful. 'Maybe it's Michael Jackson!'

His big sister scoffs, 'Michael Jackson's dead, Charlie.'

'Erica!'

'Well, he is, isn't he? You said he died when you were pregnant with me.'

I can feel her dark eyes challenging me.

'Well, yes. But still.'

I pull up to a red light and take the opportunity to lower my sun visor and check my reflection. The past few months show on my face in angry, red blemishes. I wear my mental health like a face mask. I flip the mirror back up as the light turns green. 'It's not a water park and it's definitely *not* Michael Jackson.'

Silence falls over my children, but I imagine the cogs turning inside their wonderful little minds as we drive north along Marmion Avenue—towards the surprise I've been promising for weeks. My stomach churns. I've been looking forward to this moment for months, waiting only to make sure everything was in place.

'Is it a dog?' Charlie aims higher.

Erica twists in her seat and directs a raised eyebrow at her brother in that growing-up-too-fast way she's been doing lately. 'We already have a dog.'

'We can have two, you know.'

'Yeah, doggy!' Nellie chimes in.

'You're just repeating everything we say.'

I roll my eyes, 'Come on guys, she's only three. Be nice.'

'This is taking forever.' Erica throws herself back onto her headrest, her curls fanning across her shoulders.

I sigh, 'Almost there.'

'I'm hungry.'

'Yeah, hungry!'

'Is there food there?'

'Is the surprise something we can eat?'

'Is it something we can ride?'

'Yeah, ride!'

'Is it something we can swim in?'

'Yeah, swim!'

I bite the insides of my cheeks and turn the music up. I flip through the playlist until I find something I know will distract them. I settle on BTS, and my children are

Don't Oversell It

momentarily caught up in the notion of being *smooth like butter*.

I approach the turn-off. At the sound of the indicator all three kids lean forward, craning their necks towards the front windscreen, searching for this elusive surprise.

'I'm so excited.'

'I bet it's awesome.'

'It's definitely a waterpark.'

'Yeah. park!'

I make a right turn, followed by a left, then another right. Their wide eyes follow.

Finally, I reach our destination. I park the car and turn to face my children, my smile so wide my cheeks already ache.

Three pairs of eyes stare blankly back at me: two brown and one blue.

'I don't get it!' Erica turns and takes in the sandy patch of land outside her window.

'This is it. Come on!' I exit the car and help Nellie from her car seat as the other two climb out.

Charlie toes the sand with his shoe, 'What is it?'

I open my arms triumphantly, 'This!' My heart is thumping and I feel nauseous. I spin slowly on the spot for dramatic effect. 'This is all ours, guys. We're going to build a house!' I clap with the enthusiasm of a children's show entertainer. 'Our own house!'

Nellie bursts into tears.

Charlie's face crumbles, 'I thought it was going to be something fun.'

Erica starts to walk from one side of the block to the other in large, purposeful strides. 'Are you sure it's big enough for a house? It seems pretty small.'

Heat rises to my cheeks as my jaw clenches. 'Yes. It's big enough.'

Charlie squints up at me. 'I'm still hungry. Can we go now?'

I resist the urge to scream. 'Sure.'

I scoop up my bawling three-year-old and clip her back into her car seat.

Moments later, as we pull out of the estate, Erica clears her throat. 'It's still cool, Mum.'

I force a smile through tight lips, 'Thanks, bub.'

Behind me, Charlie presses his nose against the pane of his window. 'A water park would have been better.'

'Yeah, park!'

A Long-standing Love Affair with Kisschasy

Alyssa Shapland

<u>2010</u>
Gravel dust seeps through the cracked-open windows, covering everything in a gritty, orange film. The bus hurtles along the back roads, ragged potholes sending school bags flying into the aisle. In the morning, we'd pooled our coins and decided ahead of time who would run to the tuck shop after school; the bulging paper bags of rainbow straps, piglets and red clouds passed along the seats in the afternoon. Headphone cords split and shared between ears; my iPod Nano filled with pop punk and Aussie hip-hop. Gazing out the window at paddock after paddock of apathetic cows, it's hard to imagine the world gets any bigger than these moments; mouthing along to Kisschasy songs and hoping like hell that the boy I liked would look at me someday. Spoiler alert: he didn't.

<u>2015</u>
The doors swing open and the queue edges forward. Tickets are exchanged for wristbands that inevitably stick to arm hair. Haze from the smoke machines hangs heavy in the room; the floor's already coated with spilled

vodka mixers and beer. We mill around nervously, barely touching. The support act warms up the room, gets people moving. In the break, club music blasts through speakers that shake the walls. Never mind. I'm twenty-one. Who needs hearing after this age anyway? Finally, the lights come on again, the crowd surging forward. The barrier creaks under the weight of all the enthusiasm.

Even though we've broken up, the boy I loved agreed to come with me on this ill-advised adventure. He lifts me up to stand on his feet, bolstering my weakened body with his because my joints are screaming. Something's very wrong with me, but it doesn't have a name yet. It's just a feeling; the feeling that this gig might be the last thing I ever go to. But if that's true, it doesn't matter. Nothing else matters because they're right there. On stage. It's really them. Kisschasy are in Perth and they're almost close enough to touch. The drum kickstarts my heart again, all the pain worth it for a night huddled amongst strangers, screaming lyrics to songs imprinted on my brain since I was sixteen. It's their farewell tour and it feels like an ending in more ways than one.

<u>2023</u>
In the quiet of the midnight lounge room, infant son nestled against my chest, the announcement of the decade screams at me from a Facebook post. They're going on tour again. They're coming to Perth in May and I'd sell a kidney to go. Alarms are set, plans are put in place. As soon as tickets go on sale, they're snapped

A Long-standing Love Affair with Kisschasy

up. The date is in the calendar and nothing will stop me from being there. I can't believe I've been given another chance; the chance to go to a gig and throw everything at it. The chance to scream and dance and not worry that the effort will send a fragile body into collapse.

Eight years ago, Crohn's disease had its claws in so deep that I wasn't sure I'd see Christmas. But now, after surgeries and medication and a fight that seemed impossible to win, I can stand on my own two feet. It's clear after all this time that life is far bigger than it appeared out the bus window; the paddocks and gravel long left behind in Albany. It's bigger than first heartbreak; bigger than hospital visits, struggle and pain. Instead, it's the man I love and the baby we adore. It's standing hand in hand with my sister on the sticky floor of a club, waiting for the first notes of the songs I'll never forget the words to.

When Kisschasy take to the stage, all us kids who refused to throw out our black skinny jeans crowd around the front. No matter how much time has passed, we're still the same. We might be parents, employees, serious in our day-to-day lives, but right now, in this moment, we're all sixteen again, listening to music on an old iPod, staring out the window and wondering what the future looks like.

I'll tell you now, it's pretty bloody great.

Upsy Down Town

Josephine Taylor

In the years before it began, the kids and I were busy growing in our pods of life, and we'd come together after school and over the weekends. Swimming in the ocean, and yelling as we dived beneath chops and thumpers, or floating blissfully on millpond water. Running sand into the front beach shop, often with one or two of the boys' excited friends. *Bubble O' Bill!* they'd shout and swipe their stickiness on towels as we drove home.

I was fun, yes, but I could be tough too. One hour of screens a day, that was the rule. No McDonald's if I could help it. Brown rice if I could get away with it. I wanted them to be happy, but I wanted them to value what was important. I wanted them to learn that valuing what was important could bring a contentment—a rightness—of its own.

After the rush-around of daytime, in the evenings we'd read and play games. *Lord of the Rings* and *The Rainbow Fish*. Headache and Charades. Ash's favourite wrestling game, where I had to hold on as tight as I could, never let him go. *Tighter!* he'd command, and I'd lock my hands around his wriggling body. Then songs at the side of Ben's bed. Towns that were upsy down, and that waited, many miles away, for the morning. Train whistles blowing, then stillness, and evenings winding down to just me, awake as they slept.

Remember this, I told myself sometimes. *Know how fortunate you are, and how much you love each other.*

I'm glad I lodged those moments in me; I didn't know how suddenly we'd lose them.

Because the years that followed were tough for them too, adjusting to who I became—especially in that first year, when something we all thought was temporary became fixed. The first spring segued into the first summer, and the ocean called, but the seawater took the ache to a screeching pitch, and I couldn't bear even a breeze against my body. *Philippa's coming soon*, I'd say, or, *Can you see if any of your friends are going?*

There was nothing left of me for everything else the boys needed either. I couldn't enjoy food, or read stories after dinner, or play games. Now we ate kneeling at the coffee table in the lounge room, TV permanently on, in permanently lax Sunday mode. I nodded as the boys spoke, even when I couldn't take in their words, and smiled when I could.

Ben turned nine just days after I had to stop work; he looked more to his older brother, taking his lead. Ashley turned fourteen, becoming someone I didn't know well very quickly.

Meds—ten months after the diagnosis, when I finally returned to Medico Number Seven and she wrote the new prescription—made the changes in me even stronger. The effects kicked in after Ben went to bed, and when they did, I would drop precipitately into absence. What did Ash do then? I don't know; I wasn't there anymore. Was I drooling on the sofa? Did I look old? Pathetic? Was he scared?

All I could know was him shaking me by my shoulder, urging me to go to bed. The hallway, the bedroom, then absence again, and waking to Ben at my side. They'd had their breakfast, and Ash had left to catch the bus for school. Ben would tell me his dreams, or what he would do today, and I'd drift in and out of sleep, his words now winding themselves through my dreams. I'd wake again and he'd be gone, and I'd no longer be tired enough to escape.

I don't like to think about those times, because I feel like a failure. I don't like to imagine what my sons saw when they looked at me, in case I see that version of myself. Even then, I wanted to say I'm sorry to them. Wanted to tell them, *this isn't your mother.*

It's many years ago and my boys are men and having babies of their own, but still I remember what we lost. And even now I want to go back, take myself to them somehow, square each boy by the shoulders, look into his eyes and ask him, *please don't forget me.* Tell him, *I'm still here.* We're still here.

Mistaken Identity

Sally Murphy

When my local library offers to host an event to promote my new picture book, I am delighted. For an extroverted children's author, I am surprisingly hesitant to organise these kinds of events myself—for fear nobody shows up. But if someone else does the organising, I am there with bells on.

When they contact me again a few days later to ask if I would mind, instead, going to the local school, I agree. It will save the school arranging an excursion.

'Besides,' the librarian says. 'They are really excited that you are coming to their school.'

I smile. They are excited to meet me. How lovely.

A third contact from the library. 'They are so very excited that you are coming, they are wondering if you would mind doing two sessions?' I hesitate slightly. Most author visits to schools are paid. This is a free offering, and the request for a second session is a little cheeky.

Still, they are very excited I am coming. My local school! How nice to get to share my book with the children who live in my suburb.

The day before the visit, there is a setback. A family emergency in Perth means I rush up to be there. But I am determined not to disappoint my fans. With very little sleep I drive home early on the day of my visit, fuelled by caffeine and the adrenaline of my looming appearance.

I drop into home, change my outfit to something more authorial, throw on some lipstick, grab my book bag, and dash to the school.

At the front reception I announce my arrival. The receptionist seems a little surprised. Is my sleeplessness showing? Should I have worn brighter lipstick? I am ushered towards the library.

'They are waiting for you,' I am told.

They must be very keen—I am early, as always, but it seems they are ready even earlier. I am shown through the door and enter alone.

Eighty children sit facing the front of the room. A dozen or more adults wait expectantly. No one welcomes me or introduces me. Are they cross that I'm late? Have I misread the time?

Nervous now, I make my way to the front of the room, throw my book bag down on a nearby chair, take a deep breath. I've got this. They have been eagerly awaiting my visit. I am a seasoned educator and performer.

Taking one more steadying breath, I muster every ounce of enthusiasm, and begin.

'Good morning, everyone!'

As one, the eager audience lights up. They know the response and have been practicing.

'Good morning, Sally Morgan.'

Mistaken Identity

Eighty students. Twelve adults. In unison.

My heart stops. I feel my face fall.

They have been excited about me coming.

So excited they requested a second session.

Except, not me. Sally *Morgan*. Right first name. Wrong surname.

I look to my left, where a beautiful display of books all bear the name of that other Sally.

I look to the back of the room where staff wait anxiously for me to begin.

I look at the faces of eighty children.

Is running out of the room an option? Is crying an option? Is lying an option?

I take yet another deep breath.

'Oh,' I say. 'I have a confession to make.' I swallow. 'I am *not* Sally Morgan.'

Confusion in the faces of the adults.

'I *am* called Sally. And I AM an author. But I can leave now if you like.'

Part of me hopes they say yes. But they don't. Eighty children, perhaps envisioning a too-soon return to the classroom, shake their heads and chorus 'noooo'. The adults agree, more sedately.

I reach into my bookbag, take out the book bearing my name, and start again.

Women in Waiting

Laura Motherway

An artificial plant rests plump and green in a sunlit corner. A living plant could certainly have thrived in this environment. I wonder why they chose this replica.

Across from me, a woman and her husband sit in silence, anxiety tethering them as their hands entwine. A quick glance at a mobile phone indicates this is still real life, and these are real people.

A woman and her daughter both flick through magazines, obviously not reading. Unconsciously, they finger the edges of the pages. They exude the illusion of calm, a deliberate nonchalance, but I know there's a symphony of panic that threatens to crescendo beneath the façade they seem so committed to maintaining.

I scan the room, trying my best not to be too obvious. Resisting eye contact to uphold the privacy we all hope to maintain inside these walls. In every corner of the room, a woman with her person. A partner, a child, a friend or lover.

I am alone. Solitude is my partner in this journey, and I am glad for the silence it affords me. I have nobody to ask the receptionist *how much longer?* Or to squeeze my hand uselessly as if to say *I'm sure there's nothing to worry about.*

I retreat into my daydreams again, as I have done since this journey began. I imagine a vivid world, where I am myself, but different. I am unscarred, unmarked, and whole. The person I dreamed I would be when I was a small child. I flourish in this different world, different career, different lover, different achievements. My daydreams bring me comfort and respite from reality. But I walk a fine line, never allowing myself to be lost to them. I am, after all, expected to remain … inspirational.

Collectively, we panic to avoid making eye contact with the couple who have returned from the hallway. The man pays the bill, as the woman wipes her eyes with the sleeve of her jumper and stares vacantly towards the ceiling fan. I can tell she is doing that technique where you push your tongue into the roof of your mouth to stop yourself from crying. I do it too. Not for myself, but for her. She looks younger than me. I know what's coming next for her. Her husband will try to minimise the information they have just received by pointing out how much worse it could be. She will silently stare at her hands as he fumbles through feigned pragmatism to arrange plans for meals, and childcare: that's if they are lucky enough to have a child already, because if not, this disease has taken that from her as well. He will interpret her silence as agreement, and he will be mistaken. He won't understand when she erupts screaming at him about how he could never possibly know what she is going through, and that he has no right to downplay what's happening in her body. At least she'll have her daydreams.

Then it's my turn.

I'm always intrigued by how someone can smile so genuinely when they have spent their day delivering information like this. But today's smile is brighter than usual. His hands tap at the keyboard of his computer as he says a blur of words of which I only register a few. *Successful, clear margins, nil disease detected, cured.*

I shake his warm hand and thank him with genuine gratitude. I mutter something about wishing him the best and make my way to my car.

As my seatbelt clicks into place, I remove my tongue from the roof of my mouth and release a landslide of tears, not for myself, but for the women still waiting in that room.

Canon

Caitlin Prince

On the weekend, Andy and I slow-danced in my kitchen. We read our books on my sunny balcony, surrounded by kangaroo paws bobbing in the breeze. She taught me to play guitar. And she loved me. Loved me with her eyes radiating joy as I babbled excitedly about a new mentor, loved me by sleepily enfolding my body in hers in the early hours, loved me with her fingers stroking my knee absentmindedly through torn jeans. Loved me in a whole and steady way.

On Monday morning, a student in my classroom shared her Catholic values about the queer community. In her eyes, our love is a moral evil. Her declaration hit hard and froze in my chest. I was the teacher and she the student, but a part of me suddenly shrank small. The next minutes were slow and heavy, every eye of every student on me and my rainbow lapel pin. Take care, I thought, don't … Don't what? Reveal how painful her words are to me? Don't confront too directly this belief that any which way I try to stretch it seems cruel? Don't … be gay?

My student could not know her words were nothing new, rather a repeat of the Christian communities I grew up in. An abomination, the Bible said. *Love the sinner, hate the sin,* my best friend said. *I just want your life to be easy,* Mum said. I can still see the post-box through the windscreen of my stalled car on the ordinary day I quietly resolved, *Well, I guess I should choose men,* and set off down the straight and narrow road for a long stretch of empty years. By then, the choice was abstract anyway. Though I'd been falling for women since I was twelve, I did not recognise what I felt as desire. Society had decided it was immoral to show women loving women, so wanting a woman was only ever shown to me through a male gaze: boobs in a skimpy red bikini on a size six body, skin shining like plastic and her face a blank canvas. It resembled nothing of how I felt about women.

There was no rom-com movie, no episode of *Friends,* or *Dawson's Creek* or *The OC,* that showed that feeling—when a woman talks and is smart, articulate and funny, and all the gravity in the room piles on top of you and the floor opens up and you want to puddle around her and hope she never stops talking. I did not see on screen the longing to reach out and touch a woman, not because she is a certain shape or size, but because she is *her.* No one showed the yearning I felt to reach out and ease things for another woman—cup her calf, her hip, her breast—to hold her, because she is beautiful and life is hard. There was nothing in the books in my school library about the desire to have a woman run her fingers through my hair, pull me close, draw my face near to hers so I can see I am *known* by her. These

Canon

yearnings were not shown, were not named, and instead stormed inside me, seething and secret, because society had decided this kind of love was evil.

I did not tell my student this, because I was *taking care*—of her or me, I couldn't tell.

I did go home and cry with Andy. She held me and cupped my hip and drew my face to hers so I could see that I am known by her. Later, when we walked down the street hand in hand, people smiled at us and I was reminded that the world is changing, has changed, since those adolescent days when I needed the language that nobody was stocking my library with. When we got home, I pulled out a pen to write a contribution so we can all know how women love women.

The Second Frog

Judd Exley

My brother swings the mallet at the bumper on top of a yellow metal bar as I look down at the large green rubber frog in my hand. I can't believe I'm doing this.

He's fourteen and frequently decides what we're doing when we go to visit our mother. She's taken us to a massive mall with an arcade that takes up an entire section. I'm six years younger and suck at games. I'm too anxious to try them or to give them my all. The prospect is terrifying.

He gives the mallet a mighty swing, but the short tether limits his wind-up. The lever hits the launching bowl, and the second of his two frogs flies feebly toward the tiny flower-shaped cup in the middle before falling short. Another failed attempt. It's my turn.

The prize is a giant teddy that nobody *ever* wins. I would never have wanted to play in a million years, but my mother insisted we both get a try. My brother agreed, thinking that after a failed attempt I would quit and disappear somewhere while he took my turn. That's precisely what I'd intended to do.

I place my frog, but my brother quickly leans over to tut-tut me and position the frog 'properly' like it's ready

The Second Frog

to jump. He gives our mother a smug, clever smile. I had seen him watching the young tradie before him setting up his girlfriend's frogs the same way.

I step up. The mallet's heavier than I thought, and I struggle to lift it. I make the horrid mistake of glancing around and see that there is a crowd around the Frog Pond. Fifty eager faces watch in the dim lighting as I take my swing. A weak plunking noise and the metal lever proves heavier than expected, barely knocking the bowl forward and dumping the frog weakly onto the floor, well short of the water.

Laughter rips through the crowd. The attendant is doubled over and howling and the young tradie sprays a mouthful of soda. My brother is laughing, and my cheeks get hot. My mother is laughing, and the tears start. She catches herself and I want to die.

'C'mon kid,' the attendant says, 'You can do this.'

'Yeah!' shouts the tradie, 'You've got this.'

I just want out of there. The next frog lies upside down in the bowl like he's already died from embarrassment. I grab the mallet and find that the tether is the perfect length for my little arms to get the wind-up the bigger people were trying to get. I swing with all the anger and embarrassment of the moment.

That frog arcs perfectly into the middle lily pad. I've won. The tradie's arms shoot into the air in triumph. The attendant grins as if he's just seen someone achieve the impossible. The entire place cheers. My mother hugs me and the giant bear is mine.

The Timekeeper

Ana Brawls

I sat primly on the leather lounge, waiting; trying not swing my legs. The tick-tocking of the grandfather clock echoed in the silent house, its silver pendulum the only motion. The imposing piece released one majestic note announcing it was thirty minutes past ten in the morning.

As if on cue, the air filled with the sweet aroma of *mate* tea.

'Ana Paula,' came a quiet summoning.

I skipped off the couch at the voice of my favourite grand-auntie Cida. On the table: a cup, a saucer, home-made bread, and a pot of tea. She poured me tea and sliced the bread. Breaking it into small pieces, her soft, wrinkled hands submerged the chunks into the cup with such gentleness that a tiny undulation was the only indication the surface was ever broken. The sweet tea infused the bread, softening it to a comforting texture.

We called it 'bread soup'.

I spent most of my afternoons with the unmarried siblings of my late grandfather, who lived across the road from us. In this house, I reigned supreme. Neither my siblings nor cousins ever shared this privilege. None of

The Timekeeper

them were ever educated on Friday afternoons by a hired matron on sewing or etiquette. None of them performed pirouettes before her watchful, hawk-like eyes.

I grew up watching my aunties powdering their faces and tying their hair, hiding it under small scarves, before leaving the house to run errands. Not much different from the peasants who worked the fields of their youth. I marvelled at the reverence they displayed while unfurling their silk stockings, along their old, dry coffee-coloured legs.

They created and sewed everything they wore.

The second oldest auntie, Alice, and I would play hide-and-seek. But I loved it best when we played school.

I pretended to be the teacher. Alice would sit with a scrap of paper in hand, her hunched back prominent, and I would teach the alphabet like I had learned at school. Then, I would teach her how to spell her name, as if she was in first grade.

Later in life, I learnt that this was the only education she ever had.

The four women shared a large room, fitted with four single beds, likes the dwarves in Snow White. There was a separate room for my reclusive uncle. He only came out on three occasions: to eat, to pray, and to wind the grandfather clock.

Uncle Jose would collect a long, shiny key hidden atop the clock, unlock its glass door and wind it with that same key until he couldn't wind it anymore, or perhaps he was just happy with its calibration. He would lock the door, place the key back in its rightful place and, without uttering a word, make his way back upstairs to his room.

His bedroom was like a secret chamber. Brazilian hardwood decorated the compact space. Strangely, what attracted me the most was the distinguished smell of tobacco. I used to sit on top of his wooden chest watching him rolling it on straw. He would admire his handiwork before standing up and lighting it by the window. His small portable radio would be playing classical music in the background.

More often than not, I would use his wardrobe as a hiding spot, the double doors had a key each. I would unlock one and squeeze inside, where his suits and boxes shared the minimal space. But my favourite hiding place was the dark wooden chest; big and imposing. The keyhole was always empty and it was never locked. My uncle never once stopped me from playing there.

My aunties kept the reminiscence of their past lives there—hats, fabric, doilies, towels. Along with the furniture and utensils, they were the only remains of our family's coffee farm.

Years later, when I was in my second year of law school, my mother called me with news of Uncle Jose's passing, saying I shouldn't come as he was going to be buried that afternoon.

Who would turn the key and keep time going? I like to imagine the clock ticking away, quietly and calmly, only making itself known when necessary, a bit like my uncle.

The Beginning of the End

Claire Stewart

'I'm in Hinderwell Street in Scarborough, can you come and pick me up?'

'What are you doing there?'

'I'll explain later.'

I hung up, annoyed that my father had escaped from his hospital bed at one o'clock in the morning and expected me to play St Bernard.

It was July, there was no wind crackling or muffling the mouthpiece and I could not hear any traffic in the background. Hinderwell Street was close to a major road, a few streets back from the ocean. He was lucid and not complaining about the cold. To save myself the trouble of getting out of my pyjamas and driving to the other side of Perth to a block of flats that have long since been demolished, I contacted the after-hours line at the hospital. I was put on hold.

The nurse returned a few minutes later. He was in his bed and fast asleep.

'If I ever get to the stage where I am unable to wipe my own arse,' he tells me in between grunts of chin-ups that he does to work twice as fast as men half his age, 'I want you to put me out of my misery.'

'If I get to the stage where I don't know where I am or who I used to be,' he muses while shifting to third gear on his 1972 Volvo that he has kept alive for the last ten years from the discarded parts of others, 'you have permission to put a pillow over my head.'

'If I am ever in a position that I can't move or look after myself,' he says while sanding down the king-size bed he built before moving out and starting a new life, 'and you don't pull the plug, I will spit on you. You are not going to look after me.'

He dreamed about going to New York and Scotland when he had the money. Over time, his dream destination became Switzerland.

'Purgatory is for Catholics,' he muttered in frustration when the car ahead of him hovered between two lanes, unable to decide whether to exit onto Vincent Street or continue onto Kwinana Freeway.

When I see him now, he tells me that he is going to visit his mother and grandmother. He points to where they are staying from his window. Other times he will tell me he is going to the shops, or he is going to escape because he can't stand the food here. He is relieved to see me come at 5 pm on a Friday with a Thai takeaway because he *cannot stand another Friday of fucking fish*.

'You're not Catholic,' I joke. I play him his favourites from his era like Leonard Cohen and Janis Joplin and

The Beginning of the End

his favourites from mine like Angus and Julia Stone and PJ Harvey. Most of the time we watch TV. Anything to drown out the sounds of the old ladies and carers singing 'Side by Side,' 'All Things Bright and Beautiful' or, god forbid, 'Que Sera Sera'. Or the cries of the elderly woman asking God to please kill her because she has had enough.

It's hard not talking about the things we used to do, but not as hard as waking up from the dreams where he is walking again, as though his paralysis was only temporary, and he would bound out of his wheelchair like Lazarus and come home with me. I feel guilt constantly. Did I listen to him as attentively as he listened to me? Was I patient with him? Did I ignore any signs? He was a sixty-seven-year-old man who drove a car, did woodwork and made pumpkin soup. In three short years he was immobile, barely speaking more than a few short sentences and thinking it was 1979. I'm waiting for him to ask where his two-year-old daughter has gone, not realising she is the middle-aged woman in front of him.

He never made it to New York or Scotland. It's too late to go to Switzerland. I can't put a pillow over his head or put him out of his misery. I haven't pulled the plug and he hasn't spat on me, yet.

He is not Catholic, but he is in purgatory.

My First Apple, 1954

Serge Toussaint

Apples did not grow in Mauritius when I was a child. There were of course the *pommes jacot,* better known by their creole name of *pommes zaco,* or *monkey apples;* a type of crab apple that puckers the lips and screws the eyes shut. Real apples only came from Australia or South Africa. They were exorbitantly expensive.

It was an absolute treat when Papi, our father, came home from work and solemnly announced: 'Tonight we shall have apple for dessert! Apples are usually far too pricey; today, they were affordable.' I thought he meant one apple for each one of us: himself, Mamie our mother and *les cinq grands,* the older five, which, of course, included me, the fourth in line of their ten children. It seemed to me totally appropriate that he should exclude *les cinq petits,* the five younger ones, from the count; they might well have choked on an apple core.

I could not have been more mistaken. That day, Papi was referring to one apple! Yes. One apple for seven of us. From that day onwards, 'Apple for dessert' meant one and only one apple to be divided amongst seven of us.

The carving of the apple was quite a performance. At the end of the meal, once the table had been completely

My First Apple, 1954

cleared and all crumbs dusted away, Papi would place the sacrificial apple on a special plate in front of him. He would pick it up carefully with his fingertips and present it to us with a great sense of pride, like a trophy. Awestruck, we would watch in silence until Papi finally carved The Apple, ceremoniously and meticulously, into eight very precise segments.

'Why eight segments, when there were only seven of us at the table?' A fair question; one for which Papi always had the answer. After handing over a small segment of the coveted apple to each one of us, he would say, as if taken totally by surprise: 'Oh! There's one piece left over. It must be mine.'

I used to long for the day I would be able to afford a whole apple; one that I would enjoy all by myself. I was ten years old when that memorable day arrived. Even though Eve and the famous apple of the Bible do not figure in the story, the occasion did have a religious component to it. It was on a day when the primary school I attended went on a pilgrimage to the well-known shrine of Marie Reine de la Paix in Port Louis, the capital of Mauritius. I had saved my pocket money for several weeks; it may even have been months. When we boarded the train that morning, I had in my school bag a huge, shiny, red apple from Australia. My own apple.

Several times during the journey, I took the precious apple out of the bag just to admire it, smell it and give it an extra polish.

At the shrine, I could not concentrate on mass, pray or listen to the sermon. No religious ceremony had ever seemed so unbearably lengthy. It could not end soon enough. I must confess that the relief I felt when it was all over did bring on a tiny twinge of guilt. But not enough to spoil the unforgettable moment when I took a huge bite of that delicious, juicy apple from Australia.

Helicopter Parents

Guy Salvidge

Our son is on a helicopter, my ex-wife Gina texts me.
 Awesome, as long as not for rescue purposes, I text back.
 He paid for it. He just texted it didn't crash.

It's 31 August and our sixteen-year-old son Leon is on a school excursion to Dowerin Field Day, an annual farming expo. He lives in Northam with me, my wife Narissa, and five-year-old Ronan. This morning I dropped Leon off at school before heading down to Perth to give a tutorial at Curtin University. By early afternoon, we're 160 km apart.

It doesn't occur to me to be worried, the Sea World helicopter tragedy earlier in the year notwithstanding. Leon is safely back on terra firma and makes it home from Dowerin, and meanwhile, I successfully navigate what a work colleague once infamously dubbed Death Road.

At home, Leon explains that the flight cost him eighty dollars and lasted about fifteen minutes and that while it was interesting, he doesn't think it was worth the money. I tell him it's an experience he'll remember for a lifetime and that he'll have forgotten about the money within a week.

That's about as far as our conversation goes before Narissa and I have to rush out to hand in the Japanese sashiko quilt she's entering into the York Show. Entries close at six and it's five now, and the drive takes thirty minutes. We pile Narissa's quilt, Ronan and his remote-control cars into the station wagon and off we go. No sooner do we get underway, than my phone starts ringing. The screen flashes up Josie, the new principal at Leon's school. The school where I have worked for sixteen years.

'Answer it,' I say.

Narissa answers my phone and puts it on speaker.

'Hi, Josie,' I say. 'How are you?'

Josie is a month into her stint as principal, but we know each other from when she was my boss in English years earlier. To my mind, this call can only be about the promotion for which I've recently applied. Could it be that I've got the job already?

'Did Leon go on a helicopter today?' Josie says.

'Yee-eees.'

'I see. And did he have parental permission?'

'No-oooo.'

Narissa interrupts me. Furious discussion ensues. Turns out *she* gave Leon verbal permission, or at least he called her before the fact. Turns out he called Gina too. I convey this to Josie.

She exhales. 'All right then.' And ends the call.

Further discussion occurs, in which I begin to form the opinion that Leon oughtn't to have gone on

Helicopter Parents

that bloody helicopter. Look at it from the principal's perspective. An unscheduled *helicopter ride* while on an official school excursion? While under the school's duty of care? Just think of the paperwork if the damn thing had crashed. I can only hope this doesn't adversely affect my prospects.

Later, the sashiko quilt in under the wire (it wins first prize), I discuss the helicopter matter with Leon. At length. What I can't fathom is how a company can allow a student in full school uniform to ride their helicopter without written parental permission or a signed waiver. He doesn't even have an invoice beyond the EFTPOS receipt to prove it ever happened.

'No one had a problem with it,' he says.

'No one except the principal,' I say. 'You can understand why.'

He can. The root cause of the problem, we can all agree, is the way Leon has been raised. Having me for a father has taught him not to follow rules slavishly or to shy away from circumventing authority when it suits. Having me as a father has made him the kind of guy who gets on a helicopter just because he wanted to and no one told him no.

I ring Gina and soon everyone is sick of hearing about the helicopter. We agree that while she isn't to blame, Leon certainly isn't either, and the only way anyone's pinning it on me is by way of some greater moral failure. We raised our son to think for himself, didn't we?

Turns out neither of us are helicopter parents.

The Mustard Pot

Rosemary Sayer

I stare at the broken pottery shards spread around the kitchen tiles with horror. It was only an old, glazed mustard pot with an ill-fitting lid and wooden spoon, but I remember my mother laughing in the crowded summer market of Provence as she held up her find like a piece of rare treasure.

'Just the thing for your kitchen,' she told me.

Now, years later, those shattered pieces seem to reflect my loss more deeply. Crying, I keep telling myself it doesn't matter, it was only an old mustard pot—just 'a thing' that I could easily replace. But it was something tangible that my mother and I had bought together on one of our shared holidays. Such a simple thing really, but I used it most days in France when I filled my baguette with ham and tomato before spreading a layer of mustard and joining the two halves of bread.

When someone dies, all that remains are memories. For me, touching and using my mother's things strengthen those memories best; filling my cup from one of her coloured teapots, pinning on her brooch or simply running my hands over the soft wool of the jumpers and rugs she knitted for me. I like these physical, tactile

The Mustard Pot

reminders of her pouring, pinning, or knitting. She is alive in that moment, telling me to empty the tea leaves onto the mint in the garden, carefully closing the clasp of an antique brooch on her jacket or smiling at me from a comfortable armchair with wool spilling onto her lap and into a knitting basket at her feet.

So even though I will replace the mustard pot, and I might even find an old one with a yellow glaze and funny lid, it won't be the same. It won't be the simple thing that I held in my hand at a market in Provence with Mum.

Waterfall

Joel Huey

There's a special place in the Gulf Country, past a roadhouse named for dead explorers, at the end of a dirt road that chews tyres and shatters windshields. A place where ridges erupt from grassy plains. Where chocolate billabongs turn to clear flowing water.

It's not on the way to anywhere. And if you don't like flies, you'd rather be anywhere else. The drinking water makes your guts cramp, and the camp sites are raked dirt. But here, a long and dusty walk from the car, is a special place.

Indarri Falls pours over a wall built by subterranean water. Most water erodes, grinding rocks into mud over millennia. Here, the water builds. By a quirk of chemistry, dissolved minerals are extracted from deep underground and deposited at the surface to create rocks. The foamy sheet of the falls hides a smooth limestone platform, built and polished by mineralised water pouring through the roots of the shady trees above.

I first sat on this hidden rock when I was thirteen, shrouded by the falls, while watching archerfish shoot insects from low-hanging branches. I knew it as Lawn

Waterfall

Hill, a beautiful oasis nestled in the expansive savannah. When you overlook the emerald waters snaking through red gorges, you see why it has always been called Boodjamulla—Rainbow Serpent Country.

Under those falls, I fell in love.

For a small boy, the park rangers were like adventurers. Their confident lectures on plants and animals were full of dry humour. They showed me how to manage the flies, by letting them settle around my eyes and mouth. They told wild stories of hunting pigs and donkeys at the water's edge. They were living and working in isolation to conserve this delicate ecosystem.

I wanted to join them. The flies and dust seemed like a small price to pay to feel embraced by nature. Here I could live a life of purpose and excitement.

My path was set, I would return.

Ten years later, my life had carved a new path. I had pursued my studies diligently, going from school to university, routinely checking the government job board for 'ranger AND Lawn Hill'. Somewhere along the way I was diverted. The passion to conserve was funnelled into a need to understand. I kept studying.

We were budding ecologists. Jimmy was older. His journey had taken longer, but here we were, together in big sky country. We sailed across the sea of brown grass, blasting *War of the Worlds* and Robert Miles, the Landcruiser's tiny speakers struggling with the bass. We had the sort of friendship where trivial arguments could amuse us for hours as we netted catfish and dug up mussels. However, after ten days on the road, the heat and work were grinding us down. We needed a diversion, we needed to recharge.

Jimmy and I swam across the same pool I had when I was thirteen years old. I felt the same vertigo, looking down through clear water that faded from dark green into black. I idly watched the same archerfish, who I could now name in latinised Greek.

We sat together on the rock, the small irritations of working and camping washed away. We sat in silence, listening to the falling water.

'I was here about ten years ago, with my girlfriend,' Jimmy said. He sounded sad; I knew that relationship had been important. Fieldwork gives you lots of time to share.

'I was too.'

Jimmy knew my story. How my family had lived in a bus for a year, travelling across the country, while my brothers and I did school by mail. How we had visited this place briefly before my brother got sick because of the water. How my path had been set on this rock.

We were silent again, lost in the journeys that had brought us here.

Horse

Theresa Wilks

I'm screaming at the injustice. 'How come I don't get to ride the horse?' A pertinent question, and quite eloquent I think, for a three-and-a-half-year-old, as I'm being dragged by the arm back to the family car.

Mum and Dad had stopped at a friend's farm in Australind. The place where the paddock had been located is now buried under the asphalt of a shopping centre car park, but back then horses were lined up, saddled, and tied to a post-and-rail fence surrounding an old weatherboard house. It was just across the road from the BP fuel station—which is still there today—and a tiny wooden church where I had just spent an uncomfortable hour in my scratchy lace dress for Sunday best. The farmers were giving pony rides for the congregation's children after church.

My brother, eighteen months older than me, was being led around on an old grey horse with large black eyes and ears that moved languidly back and forth. When they returned to the fence and my brother was set back on the ground, my father bent and lifted me up to sit in the saddle. Mum moved closer.

The earth around me seemed to move as the horse flicked her tail and stomped at the flies, and the smell of horse and leather filled my head as I grasped a handful of her mane waiting for my ride.

But Mum said 'no,' and I cried out as Dad lifted me back down. 'You're too small,' said Mum, then, 'Stop that noise and do as you are told! You'll get your dress dirty.'

I'm still sobbing intermittently as I get into the back of the car and sit next to my brother, my body tight with indignation and rage. He is serenely watching the other children lining up for their pony rides.

Later at home, Mum puts me to bed. She says I'm just overtired and need some sleep. As I lie there awake, I start this new thing where I can do anything I want. When I'm older at school, my teachers berate me for staring out the windows and not paying attention, but nothing soothes my rage at the world so much as imagining it a different place to the one I must inhabit.

So, I lie in my bed and feel the earth move as the horse flicks her tail and turns her head before stepping around to follow the woman holding a lead rope. I feel the coarse hair within my fists pull tight as I regain my balance—my short legs poking out either side of the wide saddle. An utter joy infuses my body as I watch those ears flip forwards and backwards. She smells of earth and sweat. Her head nods rhythmically to the slow thud of her hooves and my little heart lifts up to the top of the world.

Collaboration with Light

Emily Rainsford

'I feel like I'm in a tunnel and I can't see the light at the end of it,' I said to my partner, arms full, boobs full, heavy.

I had longed for a baby for longer than I'd been an adult. The thing about babies is that you can never love them too much. They will never tell you that you're too much, that your love is too much. It never once occurred to me, in all those aching, heart-overflowing-but-no-takers years, that I wouldn't have enough.

I didn't know that the labour of love could be soul-deep trauma. I didn't know that after five long, pelvis-torn days, my dreams of the idyllic home birth would lie in pieces on a hospital-room floor. I didn't know that my body would be wracked with tremors while, epidural-dull, I felt like I was watching it all from somewhere else as my body prepared to eject everything that had held me hostage the past nine months.

'Have you fed her yet?' asked a nurse brusquely a few hours later as we were preparing to go home. Was I supposed to know how? Turns out the womanly art of breastfeeding, that beautiful instinct, starts out with a nurse grabbing your boob in one hand and a little stranger's head in the other, and ramming them together like two stubborn pieces of Lego. I wondered when I was going to start feeling more like this was my life and less like I'd been *Freaky Friday*-ed into someone else's.

They say endings are beginnings. But that means beginnings are endings too. Everyone expects you to celebrate this little beginning, with little beginning fingers and little beginning toes. But no one ever asks how you're coping with the ending, the ending of the woman you were before. Everyone expects you to be on cloud nine—no one asks if you're mourning the life that's now nine feet under. Your life—the one that was. No one prepares you for the tunnel, or that your stumbling through it will be devoted solely to the needs of someone else, and that everyone will expect you to think it's beautiful, while you squint, arms-full, desperate for just the tiniest spark of light.

One day I picked up a camera. Cameras work by collecting light and using it to paint a picture in the darkness. When you click the shutter, light rays dance with whatever is in front of it and speak their truth onto silver or sensor. It's a collaboration—between the eye and the finger and the camera and the light—a collaboration of light.

A camera knows that there's light in the most ordinary of things. It sees the way golden evening rays bounce off baby bottles or wispy curls. It notices the sweet innocence of a sleeping face, the relief of an hour's peace. Seeking places to point my lens taught me to see even the tiniest of sparks—even in dark tunnels. Those sparks were the breadcrumbs, and I followed them like Gretel clawing her way out of the woods, collecting them with my memory card—my light saver, my life saver.

I haven't picked my camera up in years. I can see the light on my own now. The light that bounces off two growing bodies, two sets of trusting eyes, off school badges and love-you-mum drawings and silly jokes about poo. Off the butterfly in the mirror, the woman-after, the mother.

Turns out it wasn't a tunnel at all. It was a chrysalis. And one day it cracked open and all the light came in.

The Man on the Driveway

Maria Papas

Friday sunset, and the man is sitting on a plastic chair at the edge of his driveway again. I guess him to be ten or so years older than my dad, but he doesn't seem as free in his movements, and the regularity with which he comes outside to sit like this strikes me. In our neighbourhood we're park after park, and two national reserves. We're bush tracks all the way to the beach. Lake on the other side. A shopping centre a few streets back. There are so many places to explore. Yet most nights, he sits on the same grey chair, at the same spot on his driveway, with the same stereo sound of Gregorian chants behind him. He waves when I jog past. He waves, and then he watches the changing colours of sky.

It bothers my father when I mention him.

I hope that never happens to me, he says, and I wonder what it might've once been like for this man, when instead of sitting alone at the edge of his driveway, he might've had someone, and they might've easily walked the 200 steps down the road to the reserve. How together

The Man on the Driveway

they might've witnessed sunsets so vast they stretched across 180 degrees of ocean.

Monday morning, and now I'm the one to watch the world at a distance. From inside my balcony doors, I can see across most of the lake. Today the fog is heavy, and although it makes a beautiful sunrise, there's a clear and uninviting chill to the glass. Outside, someone wheels their bins in, and it takes me back to a time when the children were young, and when the eldest would make such a fuss over rubbish day. How he'd run at speed to the front yard just to wave at the truck, cornflakes soggy inside. He would've hated being a toddler here: bins finished and gone before the sunrise.

Downstairs, I hear my father whistle, and I know already there'll be fresh bread on the benchtop, and the newspaper from his first outing of the day. Every morning up and moving, and now the sound of him unloading the dishwasher, whistling, humming. There are tunes that come with the beat of my own childhood: country and western, blues, folk from villages and places long gone. Soon enough too, there are tunes that break into songs specifically designed to irritate my mother into waking. Love songs mostly. Songs featuring her name.

I hear the tap water running. I hear the base of a small saucepan as my father places it onto the stove. I hear the almost simultaneous clicks of both the kettle and the toaster.

He calls my mother.

The sound of her name again, but this time in Greek.

The sound of him counting the minutes to boil eggs for his breakfast and for hers.

18,000 steps: that was his other count yesterday. 12,000 the day before. 16,000 on Friday. Over and over. He and my mother—as timed and as predictable as the sun itself, and the lift of fog, and the boy who runs outside each Wednesday to catch the bin truck.

Now I hear my mother's footsteps pad sleepily down the hallway.

I hear the lift and placement of a bar stool.

My father's voice.

My mother laughing at something he just said.

In front of me, I can see that the glass on the balcony doors needs cleaning, everything spotty from recent rains. I think how later my parents will synchronise their day, how they'll head out to potter in the garden, how they'll have morning tea together and maybe take a wander to the shops, and how when they return, they might see me struggling to wash these windows and ask if I need a hand. I think about how later on, they'll check their steps and decide to walk just that little bit more, maybe around the block, or up through the reserve with the limestone paths and the trees and the aspect of the ocean that reminds my mother of the aspect she had growing up in Greece.

The Man on the Driveway

How in the evening I might walk or jog too. And how I'll come around the top of the hill and look for the man who every night sits at the edge of his driveway.

How I'll buckle over breathless. If I see his chair, empty.

Learning to Swim

Asha Rajan

When you are a child, you learn to swim. You fill your lungs and submerge, releasing your breath in corpulent bubbles that fizz to the surface. You learn to tilt your head to alternate sides when you take a breath, learn to breathe after odd—not even—strokes so your neck doesn't develop a crick, pace your breaths so you aren't dizzy from flinging your head from side to side. You learn to slow your heart, steady its rhythm, push it back down from your throat where it pulses, ready to leap out, taking the contents of your stomach with it. You learn to tune out distractions.

You remember this when, at thirteen, a man follows you from your dance rehearsal in the city, down quiet laneways to where your father is waiting in his car. You turn your head on every fifth step, sneaking glances over your shoulder as if you've pulled ahead in a race. You push your heart back down, emerge onto the main street and clamber into the safety of your father's car.

You remember again at eighteen when your father is given a prognosis of three to six months to live, with

Learning to Swim

a promise of treatments that will wrack his body and shatter his courage. You sit with him in hospital between university lectures or hole up in the library to read medical journals. You tune out distractions. You keep swimming.

You remember once more at twenty when a boy gets your phone number from a friend of a friend and calls you. Repeatedly. Until you agree to go out with him once, heart pulsing in your throat, hoping you'll make it back. You breathe. You slow your heartbeat. You don't see him again.

You remember to inhale and exhale when your father, who survived his prognosis by five years, is visited once more by malefic demons clawing at his lungs. You are practiced at this stroke. You slip through hospital corridors, glide through specialist appointments. At 3 am by the edge of his bed, his body folded in half as his lungs betray him, you breathe with him. He survives another five years.

When he dies, you forget how to breathe. Two weeks later, your first pregnancy ends. There is not enough oxygen in your lungs.

When years later, your first-born falls into the quagmire of depression, self-medicates, doesn't sleep, you inhale and exhale in measured breaths. You learn survival strokes.

When your first-born disappears, leaving a note and a kiss, your lungs empty. There is no air in your lungs. There is no air anywhere. You keep your head above the waterline thanks to the lifebuoy of your second-born. You do not breathe again until your first-born reappears at the other end of the day. Your limbs, weak from the lack of oxygen, collapse beneath you. You forget how to swim.

For the next four years you relearn how to swim, relearn how to breathe.

Then it is your second-born's turn to self-medicate. He swims into turbulent waters, swirls into psychosis. The whirlpool drags you under, forces the air from your lungs once more. You gasp, grasp for handholds, refuse to let your progeny drown. A hand reaches for you, and for your second child. Your first-born, lungs filled with air, pulls you to the surface, lifts his brother too, swims to the shore with you both. He is a strong, confident swimmer now.

The three of you collapse on the beach, spent, the air around you undisturbed except for the rasping of discordant breathing.

Learning to Swim

The furious pounding of your hearts slow, fall into a rhythm, harmonise. Your breath steadies. Together, hands clutched tightly, you venture back to the water's edge. You wade in, take small tentative strokes, feel the water around your legs.

You will not let each other drown.

Together, you make for deep water.

The Shells

Viki Cramer

My sister and I crouch like reef herons, peering with unwavering focus into the limpid pools. After a time, one of us will jump up, blue ice-cream bucket in hand, to scamper over basalt rocks and land at the next wet depression that pockmarks the rocky platform. This is a treasure hunt. But there are rules. Dad has schooled us in the deadly ways of those who lurk under crevices. We are *never* to extend searching fingers to grasp the tapering spiral of a cone shell, not even if we're sure its deadly tenant has long since departed residence. The warnings of the small octopus, whose rings flash like the blue lights of the disco, must be heeded. We are content to let these small dangers be—they are not the treasures we desire. We seek, above all else, the speckle of a cowrie shell, its smooth curve like a quenelle of ice-cream, plated perfectly on the sand.

Above us the sandstone headland of Point Cartwright rises with the bulk of a cathedral, the new lighthouse its modern spire. Dad tells me that when the swell is running big, ahead of a storm, the prawn trawler sinks into troughs so deep that the light's beam, sixty metres above them, is eclipsed by the surging

The Shells

peaks. On nights when the lightning flashes through the thin curtains of my bedroom window, I grasp the sheet to my chin as the fear swells salty in my throat. The vision of Dad, a matchstick capped in his fluoro-orange beanie, bracing his feet on that slippery wooden deck with the mountain of water between him and the light.

* * *

Mum had kept them, after all these years. Through the family move a thousand kilometres north to the little grey-green boxes of the company mining town. Then through her lone upheaval to the humid coast when the company man told her that, with her husband's bones now twelve months in the ground, it was time to leave. The shells sit beached on the headland of the kitchen cabinetry—the best of the spotted cowries from Point Cartwright and the grand volutes Dad salvaged from the trawler's nets, tumbled together in a large glass jar. My sister and I find lesser treasures in the shed, still in blue ice-cream buckets. We have to decide what to keep, what to give away, what to discard. I get stuck on the shells. Their cocoons of calcium carbonate protect soft-shadowed voids that hold a memory of sea and sky and the best of my father; how he taught me to see—not just look at—the more-than-human world. I think about my mother, resting in the rehabilitation hospital as her hip bones heal. They are as fragile and flaking as the faded shells. How strong she was. She will never return to this house. Soon enough, she won't remember it.

Open Studio

Caroline Juniper

I unlock the door to Mum's house in Augusta—to her presence—and it smells faintly of her perfume and strongly of mothballs. It is quiet because she is not here. But there is another presence here, and I can visualize him sitting on the couch smiling at me. He loves it when I visit.

This is my place for a whole week, interrupted by visitors who may or may not buy my art. The days pass languidly in my mum's house; I think of what to have for lunch, for dinner. A glass of wine.

I welcome the silence here, and the ritual of walks along the river and to the beach with the little dog whose soul keeps me company. Birds sing and squabble in the garden; they flit and scatter when I walk out the front door.

Mum has gone on a road trip, driving from Cairns to Adelaide, with a daughter-in-law and two nephews. An adventurous, distracting escape. She swallows up her loneliness with conversation, events, happenings and travel. Anything to keep her from the absence she feels at home, in this house, without Dad. Her desolation and sadness is a gripping pain in the chest—a black bird—deep sorrow. It would be so easy to fall into a numbing heap of grief.

But Mum fights it and keeps on moving.

This is a small town, with its problems and possibilities. People stop to give my mum a hug and ask how she is. Tears flow and there's an invitation out somewhere to help her to forget.

I love a small town for a time. It feels like a storybook full of characters playing a part, as I wander around in it. A small town is a dear friend who keeps you close.

It's protection. It's Dad.

And Dad is everywhere. He passes by in his boat, when we go to the river in the late afternoon to watch the swans feed. Dad is with us on the bench sipping wine, watching the steely water and the silken sky pinken. But mostly he is in the house—laughing, giving twigs of advice, singing in the morning, lighting the fire and lighting up our hearts. That's where I am now, and someone is knocking on the door.

Editors

Laura Keenan is co-publisher and editor at Night Parrot Press. In 2002, Laura met flash fiction in a writers group in Denver, Colorado, and has been head-over-heels for the genre ever since. Her career as an editor spans twenty years, working for publishers including the Perseus Books Group (USA) and UWA Publishing. She runs flash fiction writing workshops in schools, libraries and community centres, encouraging others to obsess over small, intense stories. When she's not editing and writing, Laura dreams of one day dancing in a flash mob.

Casey Mulder is a Ballardong Noongar woman with Dutch and English heritage. She works in a variety of education roles and is also a freelance editor and writer. In 2022, she received a Creative Development Scholarship from Magabala Books to complete an editing mentorship at Night Parrot Press. Casey facilitates the First Nations Write Night at the Centre for Stories with Luisa Mitchell and is currently working on a creative non-fiction manuscript. She is also the First Nations editor for *Westerly* Magazine. Casey loves storytelling in all its forms and lives near the bilya on Whadjuk boodja.

Contributors

David Allan-Petale is a Boorloo/Perth writer whose debut novel *Locust Summer* was published by Fremantle Press. He lives near a lake with his children and wife, and rates art galleries by what he would steal.

Tess Allen is a creative writer who resides in Boorloo/Perth. When she's not working, or juggling family commitments, she can be found penning flash fiction and short stories over a cup of coffee. She is currently working on her first long-form project: a contemporary fiction story set in London.

Katherine Allum is a writer of literary fiction. Her debut novel *The Skeleton House* (2024, Fremantle Press) won the 2023 Fogarty Literary Award. American born, she ran away to London after uni, met an Aussie and married him, and now lives in Perth.

W. J. Arthur was born in Scotland. As a child, her thirst for stories became insatiable, searching to remember the obscure, the forgotten and the overlooked. On migrating to Australia, Arthur developed a fascination with understanding what anchors people—to the land, to each other and most importantly, to themselves.

Contributors

Danielle Berryman is a journalist and writer who has had breakfast with Darth Vader; got a standing ovation in the labour ward; and ran the Margaret River Readers & Writers Festival from 2011–2013. She helped set up two community radio stations and was on the FAWWA committee.

Isabelle Biondi Saville (she/her) is a creative writing student at Curtin University. Her work has appeared in *Coze*, Night Parrot Press, *Queerlings* and Powders Press. When she's not agonising over her sentence structure, you will often find her crocheting.

Based near Walyalup/Fremantle, English language–teaching professional **Nicki Blake**'s small fictions have been published online and in print. Her competition wins include Writing WA's inaugural 'Love to Read Local' contest and Globe Soup's Winter Flash. This is the third time her work has appeared in a Night Parrot Press anthology.

Kyeesha Bonney is a Wongi Noongar yorga, with family ties to Cosmo, Norseman and Pingelly. Kyeesha spent most of her life in Mandurah as the second oldest in a family of seven children. As the first grand-daughter, Kyeesha aspires to break the cycles of generational trauma for the future of her family.

Sharron Booth was born in Yorkshire, England, and now lives and works on Whadjuk Noongar land in Western Australia. Her first novel, *The Silence of Water* (Fremantle

Contributors

Press, 2022) was shortlisted for the 2020 City of Fremantle Hungerford Award and the 2023 MUD Literary Prize.

Writing has always been a part of **Jessica Bowker**'s life. She loved poetry as a child, studied English at university and works in corporate communications. Jessica writes regularly with the Indian Ocean Writers Group at Mattie Furphy House. She enjoys writing from lived experiences and is working on her first novel manuscript.

Ana Brawls is a librarian and writer originally from Brazil. Her work explores family traditions, myths, belonging, human condition and multiculturalism, often through alternative realities. Her poems and short stories appear in various publications in Australia and Brazil. She is grateful to live and work on Wadandi and Pibelmen Boodja.

Shannon Brie is an autistic writer living in Boorloo/Perth. A devotee of language and *The Simpsons* (Golden Age era, to be specific), she holds a Bachelor of Writing from ECU, is the Operations Manager for Writing WA, and credits her mother for instilling a lifelong love of reading.

Louise Burlinson is a writer who grew up in Sydney, lived in England and now calls Perth home. Lost in daydreams of other worlds, she spends her days composing poetry, short stories and flash fictions. Her works have been published in local anthologies and collections.

Contributors

Asha Burnett is a young emerging writer, who recently graduated from ECU with a double major in Creative and Professional Writing and English. She has been published in Night Parrot Press' *Three Can Keep a Secret* and ECU's *Dircksey* magazine. Asha has a particular fondness for writing Australian narratives.

A stranger in a strange land, **Jay Chesters** is the author of the best-selling book *Year of the Bear*, and various flash fiction pieces. In the wild, you'll often find Jay in Perth's bookshops, or its cafes and coffee shops, where he'll be writing and making the place look untidy.

Carmen Cosgrove is a perpetual reader who has recently put down a novel long enough to begin her own. She lives with her two kids in Perth's south, where she has found an outlet for her dream of benevolent dictatorship within a work of speculative fiction.

Ellie Cottrell is a writer and poet working on Whadjuk Noongar Country. She likes short poems too, which is reflected in her debut poetry collection *Speakeasy*. Ellie is honoured to be featured in this anthology.

Viki Cramer is a writer and ecologist whose work seeks to understand how both the human and more-than-human world can flourish in the landscapes we share. She is the author of *The Memory of Trees: The future of eucalypts and our home among them*.

Contributors

Aksel Dadswell is a West Australian writer of horror and weird fiction (and now memoir). He has a PhD, and lectures in Creative Writing at Edith Cowan University. He lives and works in the South West, dreaming up new ways to give people nightmares.

Alison Davis is a Perth writer who has fallen in love with flash. She's had works published in various Australian anthologies, including *Award Winning Australian Writing* and previous Night Parrot Press publications, and the 2023 Bath Flash Fiction Anthology. You can find her at www.alisondaviswriter.com.

Zoe Deleuil is a writer from Perth, Western Australia. Her fiction, essays and feature articles have been anthologised and published in literary journals and other places. Her debut novel, *The Night Village*, was published in 2021.

Barry Divola is a journalist, author and musician born and bred in Sydney, now living in Perth. His most recent book is the music-infused novel *Driving Stevie Fracasso*, about two estranged brothers on a road trip from Texas to New York City in the days leading up to 9/11.

K. T. Downs is a Geraldton writer of the Coral Coast in WA, on Yamatji Country. She writes short stories, and memoir, published locally. She was shortlisted in Big Sky Writers Festival 2021 and is currently working on a novel. Micro memoir is a recent discovery.

Contributors

Sabrina Dudgeon-Swift is descended from the Bardi people from north of Broome, and the Gija people in the East Kimberley. Her short stories and flash fiction writing have been published by Margaret River Press, *Westerly* and Night Parrot Press. Sabrina especially enjoys writing for children, and has been published by Fremantle Press.

Rachelle Erzay lives, works and writes on Whadjuk Country. She completed a Creative Writing Honours degree at Curtin University in 2018 and has had her short fiction feature in multiple anthologies, Underground Writers and more. Rachelle drinks too much chai, is a sucker for tragedy and can normally be found spoiling her tuxedo cat, Melisandre.

Born on a Montana mountaintop, educated in Texas and corporately careered in Colorado, **Judd Exley** then found love and became a West Australian. Published in the anthology *Like Clockwork*, he's also been longlisted in AWC's Furious Fiction and the Twisted Stringybark Short Story Award (2022), and placed second in OOTA's Spilt Ink Competition (2023).

Shannon Farrelly is a teacher and Mum of three who flies in the face of the stereotype that writers are introverts. She writes light-hearted romance and contemporary fiction with relatable female protagonists. Shannon is a collector of unfinished art projects, a Pepsi-max enthusiast, and believes Jack Pearson's the perfect man.

CONTRIBUTORS

Miriam Fisher's writing has been published in Australia, Europe and South Asia, where she wrote a book on climbing in the Himalayas. Her short fiction appears in *Limina*, *Authora Australis*, *Antithesis*, *Fudoki*, *100 Word Project*, University of Western Australia's *Lies, All Lies* and Night Parrot Press's *Twice Not Shy* and *Three Can Keep a Secret* collections.

Philippa Freegard is an analyst, researcher and editor living in Subiaco, WA. She is interested in themes of exploration (geographical and philosophical), time and memory. When she is not writing, editing or coding Philippa can often be found pacing Kings Park trying to remember the names of trees.

Jesse Galea is a checkerboard-wearing spreadsheet enthusiast whose writing has appeared in the queer speculative YA anthology *An Unexpected Party* and litmags like *#EnbyLife*, *Portside Review* and *Pulch Mag*, among others. They can be found posting countless photos of his cat and occasionally talking about books on Instagram @JesseGalea_

Mabel Gibson is a twenty-four-year-old Yamatji woman from Kinjarling/Albany. Mabel is published in *maar bidi: Next Generation Black Writing* (Magabala Books), all three NPP flash fiction anthologies and has sat on panels at various writers festivals. She hopes to one day become a publisher and provide opportunities for other First Nations writers.

Contributors

Ying Xiong (David) Goh reads and writes a lot. He enjoys good films and fancies himself a polyglot. Almost everyday, he dabbles in death and theology. Hoping one day, it'd come in handy for an anthology. Alas, dear reader, David won't reveal as much as he ought.

Tiffany Hastie is currently completing a doctorate researching animal voices in literature at Edith Cowan University. Previous two-time winner of the Talus Prize and the South West Margaret River Short Story Prize, with work appearing in *Westerly* Magazine. Tiffany's eco-fiction examines imbalances of power and grief in modern society.

Angel Hayward is a Noongar yorga with family connections to Katanning, Albany and Narrogin. Angel grew up in Perth and across regional Western Australia as the second oldest of seven children. A lover of adventure, Angel has just finished a round-the-world trip.

Caroline Hayward is an aspiring writer who wants to create stories that make people think. She loves to write about innocuous moments which have an unexpectedly profound impact like sliding doors. When she isn't reading or writing, Caroline is searching out coffee with a sweet treat on the side.

Originally from Ottawa, Canada, **Melanie Ho** is a writer based in Perth. *Journey to the West* (2017) is her short biography of Chinese opera star He Hui. Her English translation of

Contributors

Agnès Bun's *There's No Poetry in a Typhoon* was published in 2018.

Melanie Hobbs grew up in the northern suburbs of Perth, Western Australia. At thirty-six years old she still struggles to explain her cultural heritage of Singaporean, Malaysian, Tamil, and Christian roots. She teaches high school English and lives in the Perth Hills with her husband, two kids and dog.

Chrissie Horley has been writing since childhood, reawakening her passion whilst studying at Edith Cowan University. She has recently discovered the flash and micro genres, developing a keen affection for such concise writing. This is her first foray into the world of micro memoir.

Annie Horner is a retired teacher and academic. She recently completed a PhD in creative writing. The creative artefact of this doctoral thesis has been published as a book entitled *No One Was Watching*. She now resides in Margaret River.

Sharron Hough is a poet, short story writer and lover of children's literature. Born in Perth, her childhood experiences were enriched by living and attending schools in different cities around Australia. Sharron started writing as a teen and is strongly influenced by authors/poets such as Roald Dahl and Shel Silverstein.

Contributors

Joel Huey is a biologist who derives inspiration from Australian landscapes and ecosystems. A science writer for over twenty years, he recently started writing creatively, focusing on masculinity, relationships, self-discovery, and a sense of place. He lives in Roleystone, among the beautiful jarrah forest.

Greig Johnston worked as a music teacher before becoming a journalist, and he began writing fiction in his thirties. His short story 'No Through Road' was published in *Hard Labour*, an anthology of the best Australian crime fiction, and his journalism has appeared on various Australian news websites.

Caroline Juniper was born and raised in Margaret River. A retired art educator, she continues to practice as a screen print artist. Caroline's work has featured in galleries and the Margaret River Region Open Studios. She believes writing is a way of keeping memories close and vivid, much like visual art.

Grace Juniper Goodwin grew up in Margaret River, Western Australia, in a creatively driven family—her mother a visual artist and father a musician. After finishing school, Grace travelled to the city to study film as well as literature. She now resides in Victoria pursuing a career in film, but her love of writing continues to grow.

Mark Keenan lives with gratitude, on Mooro Noongar Boodja in Joondalup. Mark is a loving, supportive husband;

Contributors

caring, dedicated father; experienced mechanical engineer; amateur ultramarathon runner; and inquisitive genealogist. Mark is working on a historical literary fiction manuscript and a memoir about his alcoholism. He has been sober ten years.

Judi Lane loves life, despite it repeatedly punching her in the heart. Adoption, divorces, deaths, disease. These bruises form the basis of her writing and community education work. Her 'life writing' has appeared in *Grieve*. She lives, and laughs, in Armadale and is a member of Renegade Writers.

Martin Lindsay is a playwright, author, and notorious procrastinator of novel manuscripts, hidden away in the leafy South West town of Dunsborough. His not-so-micro fiction is published through Moody Lapcat Books. He is even known to occasionally blog at martinlindsay.net when not trying to stop local parrots from having sex on his balcony railing.

From Kinjarling/Albany, Western Australia, **Ana Lynch** likes listening to people's stories. She is a creative writing student at Curtin University. Her writing has been published in *Westerly*. Ana particularly enjoys gathering with folks of all ages to write and tell tales.

Alice Macri, a Perth local, lives near Mullaloo beach with her husband and two cats. A passionate storyteller, her creativity flourished under the influence of her grandmother, Rosie—affectionately known as G—and their shared love of literature. Alice is currently studying Creative Writing at Curtin University.

Seth Malacari (he/they) is a nonbinary trans masculine author and editor living in Boorloo. His first book, *An Unexpected Party* was published in 2023.

Shirley Marr is a first-generation Chinese Australian and author of children's fiction, including *All Four Quarters of the Moon* and the CBCA-award winning *A Glasshouse of Stars*. She describes herself as having a Western mind and an Eastern heart, writing in the space in the middle where they collide.

Donna Mazza is a writer and academic at Edith Cowan University. She is author of *Fauna* (Allen & Unwin, 2020) and *The Albanian* (Fremantle Press, 2007), winner of the TAG Hungerford Award. Her short stories, poetry and non-fiction works have been widely published in Australia and overseas.

Rachel McEleney lived in several countries before settling in the South West of Western Australia. She likes to spend time in the bush, and the Walpole landscape has inspired and appeared in most of her writing.

Kaylee McIntyre grew up in Australia, England, and Spain, uprooted across the world by the changeable moods of her father. Many people have told her, 'Your family is fascinating.

Contributors

You should write a book!' Maybe one day. Kaylee lives in Perth and works as a video news editor.

Lesley McKay was born in Queensland. With a cattle auctioneer father perhaps it was a natural choice to become an accountant and then to spend her life wanting to be an author. She lives in Claisebrook Cove.

Alastair McLean is a young up-and-coming author and recent graduate of a Bachelor of Arts in Creative & Professional Writing from ECU. Alastair's work typically explores stories of intimate connection shared between those on the fringes of society. He hopes to plant his readers in the minds of his characters.

Lauren McLennan is a passionate writer with a keen interest in micro literature. She enjoys teaching high school English, from reading stories with her students to encouraging creative writing. When not at her keyboard, Lauren can be seen exploring cafes in WA for a comfort coffee or cuddling her rescue cat.

Susan Midalia is the author of three short story collections, all shortlisted for major Australian literary awards; two novels; and a collection of short short fiction, *Miniatures*, published by Night Parrot Press. She is the co-director of the Australian Short Story Festival, now in its seventh successful year.

Contributors

Alison Middleton is a writer of contemporary fiction and other things. Originally from Scotland, she is a former journalist who has somehow managed to stay in Boorloo/Perth. She is a self-confessed massive nerd and world-class procrastinator who enjoys reading, cooking for friends and spending too much money on wine and books.

Carol Mills is a writer, artist, and interdisciplinary scholar. Carol writes in multiple genres and her creative practice is situated between the boundaries of words, drawing and painting.

Scott-Patrick Mitchell has webbed toes, which theoretically should make them a good swimmer, but alas … no. They are the author of *Clean*, which has been shortlisted in the 2023 Prime Minister's Literary Awards, the 2023 Western Australian Premier's Book Awards and the 2023 Victorian Premier's Literary Awards.

Amber Moffat writes for adults and children. Her fiction for adults has been published by *Westerly*, *Landfall* and *Overland*. Amber's poetry for children has been published by *The School Magazine*, Penguin Random House and Alphabet Soup Books/Fremantle Press. Her picture book, *I Would Dangle the Moon,* was released by MidnightSun.

Coral Montero Lopez was too busy with life and did not start reading books and writing stories until recently. Since then, she has joined numerous writing workshops. When she is not writing new stories or reading, she loves taking long walks with her dog. She works full-time as an Aboriginal archaeologist.

Sarah Moredoundt is a slightly chaotic, highly optimistic, creative communications specialist with a passion for sharing glimpses of her life through her writing. Very proud mum to two little boys and an extremely wild puppy, Sarah spends her fleeting spare moments running along the coast or visiting her favourite beaches.

Laura Motherway is a Western Australian author, poet and writer for children and adults. When she's not daydreaming up her next story, Laura is working in arts management, running children to cricket games or trying to stay sufficiently caffeinated to write just one more chapter.

Avril Mulligan is a primary school music teacher and writer from Perth, Western Australia. Her work has appeared in *Aurealis*, *Meniscus*, *Andromeda Spaceways*, *Verandah* and more. Mostly, she finds herself writing about wild places, wild hearts and impossible decisions. You can find her published stories at avrilmul.wixsite.com/avrilmulligan

Rashida Murphy writes about eccentric people and obscure sorrows. She shares her house with a multilingual cat, a monolingual husband and far too many books. She is also the author of a novel and a collection of short fiction.

Contributors

Sally Murphy is a children's author and educator who lives in the South West where she writes, reads, walks on the beach and generally loves life. Her published works include award-winning verse novels *Pearl Verses the World*, *Worse Things* and *Queen Narelle*. She can be found online at www.sallymurphy.com.au

Sean Murphy is a senior journalist producer with the ABC's flagship rural current affairs program, *Landline*. He has worked in print and broadcast media for more than forty years. He is Sydney based, but is a proud sandgroper, having begun life on Rottnest Island where his parents managed the pub.

Rebecca M. Newman writes for children and adults. You can read her work in magazines and anthologies in Australia and internationally. Rebecca is the co-editor of a 2024 poetry anthology for children, *Right Way Down*, featuring poems penned by Western Australian writers.

Ellen O'Brien (she/her) is a secondary teacher from Western Australia, where she lives with her husband and their rabbit, George. Ellen has published in *Life Writing*, History Through Fiction, and recently released a book about a fourteenth-century French pirate, *Jeanne de Belleville: The Lioness of Brittany*.

Gillian O'Shaughnessy is a writer and journalist. Her short fiction has been nominated for two Pushcart prizes and is featured in the 2023 international Best Small Fictions. She has won the London Independent Story Prize and the Fractured Literary Anthology Prize, among others. She's a submissions editor for *SmokeLong Quarterly*.

Maria Papas is the author of the award-winning *Skimming Stones,* a novel about a young woman's experience witnessing and remembering her sister's childhood cancer. In addition, she has written essays and short fiction for journals such as *TEXT, Griffith Review, Axon* and *The Letters Page*.

Tracy Peacock lives in Western Australia and writes creative non-fiction and flash fiction. A former journalist, she works in media and communications. Her work has appeared in *The Guardian Australia, The Big Issue* and *Victorian Writer*.

Rochelle Pickles is an emerging author of fiction and creative non-fiction. Her work focuses on human vulnerability, from the darkly personal to the deeply awkward. Rochelle has a background in psychology and is currently completing an MA in Creative Writing. She is working on a novel.

Caitlin Prince started writing in a palm-sized notebook when she was seven years old. She hasn't stopped. Her work has appeared in various Australian and international publications—you can google it. Right now, she lives on Whadjuk Noongar Boodja but has a penchant for moving, so google that too.

Contributors

Teena Raffa-Mulligan is a writer, reader, and daydream believer. She is a multi-published author of children's books and her short fiction and poetry has been published in magazines and anthologies. Her writing life has also included a long career as a journalist and editor.

Asha Rajan is a South Indian–Australian writer who lives and creates on Whadjuk Noongar Boodja. Her work reflects issues of culture, connection, inclusion, feminism and parenthood. Asha is perpetually curious and committed to work that demonstrates deep love and respect for First Nations people and her own cultural history. Website: asharajanwriter.com and Instagram/Threads: asha_rajan_writer

Emily Rainsford is (in no particular order) an avid reader, book reviewer, library officer, mother, chocoholic, and drinker of scalding black tea. She is the author of many pieces of poetry on scattered scraps, forgotten notebooks and deeply buried computer folders. You can find her @coffeebooksandmagic on Instagram.

Em Readman is a writer from Boorloo/Perth who explores the transient natures of queerness, self, and relationships in their writing.

Richard Rossiter is a writer, editor, occasional mentor and judge of writing competitions, with a deep interest in Australian literature. His most recent publication is *Refuge* (UWAP, 2019).

Contributors

Belinda Rowe was born in New Zealand and now lives in Walyalup/Fremantle, Western Australia with her husband and three children. In her spare time, she loves hanging out with her family in nature and writing tiny stories.

Pia Russo, first-generation Australian-born, grew up amongst a splice of Australian English and Italian words. Her confusion led to her escape into imaginary worlds. It is here she regularly resides and writes many beginnings. Wearer of many hats throughout her life's journey, she loves books, nature and dogs.

Guy Salvidge is a WA writer and teacher. He is in the latter stages of a PhD in Creative Writing at Curtin University, which means he gets to read and write all day for just a little while longer. He lives on Ballardong Noongar Boodja.

Dr Rosemary Sayer is a former journalist who has written three non-fiction books and several articles on her dual interests of human rights and creative non-fiction. She has worked as a sessional lecturer, tutor and research assistant at Curtin University. She is currently an Adjunct Research Fellow at Curtin.

Alyssa Shapland is a writer and mum from Albany, Western Australia. She has written for *The Mighty*, *Girls With Guts* and was published in the Centre for Stories collection *Journal* and Night Parrot Press's *Three Can Keep a Secret*.

Contributors

Brodi Snook is a stand-up comedian and writer. She writes for television and radio and performs all over the world. Currently living out of her suitcase, Brodi can often be found staring out the window on public transport, wondering from whence her next paycheck will come.

Dr Cindy Solonec is Nigena (Nyikina) from the West Kimberley and has lived off Country in Boorloo for more than twenty years. Married with a growing bevy of delightful grandchildren, she enjoys dabbling in writing. Cindy is the author of *Debesa,* a quintessential social history that reflects colonisation during the 1900s West Kimberley.

Claire Stewart lives in Boorloo/Perth with her three cats. She loves writing flash fiction and short stories and dabbles in analogue photography every now and again.

Josephine Taylor is a writer and editor and an Adjunct Senior Research Fellow at Edith Cowan University. Her debut novel, *Eye of a Rook* (Fremantle Press, 2021), was shortlisted in the WA Premier's Book Awards and her creative and critical writing has been anthologised and published widely.

Andrew Tetlaw grew up in the golden era of the Perth Hills when homemade pickles were common, and young kids could roam aimless and independent across hills, rivers, and valleys while their parents were oblivious.

Contributors

Ros Thomas lives for writing. She is a journalist, a TV scriptwriter, a former newspaper columnist, an author of two best-selling WA books, a speechwriter and a lover of short stories and flash fiction. Her most absorbed and passionate hours are spent arranging words on pieces of paper.

Sally Thomas is a writer and illustrator based in Perth, where she works as a copywriter and video game narrative designer. In 2022, Sally earned her first-class honours degree in English Literature. She enjoys painting and pairing art with storytelling.

Alexander Thorpe grew up in the suburbs around Walyalup/Fremantle, and has lived and worked in Georgia, China and Mexico. He is the author of two cozy mystery novels, *Death Leaves the Station* and *Death Holds the Key* (both published by Fremantle Press).

Melinda Tognini is the author of *Many Hearts, One Voice: The story of the War Widows' Guild in Western Australia* (Fremantle Press, 2015). She teaches life writing and family history at Sheridan Institute of Higher Education, works part-time for Writing WA and is currently a PhD candidate at Curtin University.

Born into a French-speaking family in Mauritius, **Serge Toussaint** migrated to Perth from London in 1974. His family had been eager to know more about his childhood. When he retired, after fifty years as a medical practitioner, he wrote several stories for their benefit. 'My First Apple' is one of them.

Emily Tsokos Purtill enjoys being part of the Night Parrot Press community. She also has fiction in *Westerly* and *Griffith Review*, and her debut novel MATIA will be published by UWAP in 2024. Emily currently writes and curates the literary subscription Kaló Taxídi available at etpliterary.com

Theresa Wilks lives on a bush block near Capel, Western Australia. She has just completed a Bachelor of Arts degree majoring in Creative Writing at ECU's South West campus. She loves writing and painting for illustration, and creates prop and set pieces for local community theatre productions. Theresa's Instagram is @twilks_writer_illustrator

Ange Yang is a Boorloo/Perth writer and reviewer. She won the 2022 SBS Diversity in Food Media writing competition. Her writing is featured in SBS Food, *WA Good Food Guide*, *Broadsheet* and *Gourmet Traveller*. She is interested in how food reconnects people with identity, place and heritage. Find her at @vegemitecongee

For more than fifteen years **Will Yeoman** was a journalist at *The West Australian*, where he occupied diverse positions including Literary Editor, Senior Arts Writer and Travel Writer. Will continues to write for The West in a freelance capacity while also regularly contributing to *Gramophone* and *Limelight* music magazines.

Flash Fiction and Micro Memoir Workshops

by Night Parrot Press

Would you like to learn how to write and edit flash fiction and micro memoir, or extend your existing skills?

We are available to come to your school, library or community centre and run our successful flash fiction and micro memoir workshops for adults, youth or children.

Our workshops focus on flash and micro forms, storytelling techniques and style, narrative structure and voice. The workshops also focus on building a supportive writing community and having fun with your writing. We have worked with and nurtured all kinds of writers, so we know how to get the best out of your writing.

Here's what recent participants have said:

> *It was a very memorable workshop—I have never learnt so much in two and a half hours!*
> —Margaret, Albany

> *Yes, the Night Parrot Press people are supportive but more importantly they make you feel brave. Just show up, learn and write.*
> —Megan, South Hedland

We'd love to hear from you. For enquiries, contact us at nightparrotpress@gmail.com

Also available from Night Parrot Press

"These are dazzling, electric stories that burst off the page with urgency and energy and linger long after the reading ... With this, their third anthology, Night Parrot Press cement their already stellar reputation as the leading publishers and teachers of flash fiction in Australia."

—Gillian O'Shaughnessy

www.nightparrotpress.com